A Dirt Cheap
(and Different) World

Offbeat Memoirs of an American Traveler
in the late 1950s and Early 1960s

Hugh Hosch

authorHOUSE®

AuthorHouse™
1663 Liberty Drive
Bloomington, IN 47403
www.authorhouse.com
Phone: 1 (800) 839-8640

Published by AuthorHouse 01/30/2016

ISBN: 978-1-5049-6838-6 (sc)
ISBN: 978-1-5049-6837-9 (e)

Print information available on the last page.

This book is printed on acid-free paper.

Twenty years from now you will be more disappointed
by the things you didn't do than by the things you did do.
So throw off the bowlines. Sail away from the safe harbor.
Catch the trade winds in your sails. Dream. Discover.

Mark Twain

I took Mark Twain's advice as a young
man. I'm so glad I did.

Hugh Hosch

CONTENTS

ILLUSTRATIONS

FOREWORD

All my life I have been "hooked" on foreign travel. Indeed, my adult life has been devoted to dreaming about, and better yet, visiting faraway places -- most of it done thanks to my travel industry profession. After getting out of the army, I went into the travel business, and I have subsequently visited over 150 countries, often with surprising happenings. This book is a collection of some of my own personal adventures during the period of the late 1950s-early 1960s – before things began really to change from what was essentially a pre-World War II world. All the stories are true. A very few of them, and some of my accompanying illustrations, have appeared previously, but the overwhelming majority are original for this book. I hope you enjoy them all.

Hugh Hosch
January, 2016

MY INTRODUCTION TO A BARGAIN (AND DIFFERENT) WORLD

A full bottle of decent wine for a dime. A room at a five star deluxe hotel in a major European city for a dollar. A shoeshine for three cents. And Indians shooting arrows at your train window in Brazil. Just a few examples of how different things could be in bygone days. When I was a young buck.

Oh, I know, inflation is nothing new. It has been felt in all countries, including the U.S., and always will be. But the price differences referred to in this book are not restricted to inflation. During the period up to twenty years after World War II, most other countries were still struggling to get their economies back on track, and the result was a bargain world for American travelers. Looking back, I was lucky to be able to see so much of the world on so little. I also realized, at the time, that I was seeing a world which would surely change dramatically in years to come, and I was eager to take in as much of it as I could, before those changes took place.

A funny memory involved the cost of a *pensión* in Granada. I had established a maximum price I would pay for a room for a night (you could haggle over the price of *pensiones*). That maximum was twenty-five pesetas, or forty cents U.S. So when I stepped off a train there and was approached by a young boy touting a *pensión*, I answered his "*Pensión, señor?*" with my standard, "*Sí, pero no pagaré más que veinticinco pesetas!*" The kid said, "*No problema!*", grabbed my small bag and set off for the place, me following. At the nearby third-floor hostelry, the lady running the place took my passport and, as required for the police, copied down my name, number, etc, then, advised by the boy that we had negotiated a price of twenty-five pesetas, the boss lady asked me for that sum (paying in advance was not unusual in *pensiones*). So I plopped down a big twenty-five peseta coin with the profile of the Generalísimo and the wording around the edge, *Francisco Franco Caudillo de España por la Gracia de Díos*, and proceeded to my room. There, on the back of the door, was posted an official notice which advised, *Precio máximo: 15 pesetas*.

In 1959 I paid the grand sum of $1.80 U.S. to journey by train 1100 miles across the relatively unknown and underpopulated southwestern part of that great region of Brazil known as the Mato Grosso, from Corumbá on the Bolivian border, to São Paulo. The ride had been fairly uneventful, other than for the ongoing little human dramas of local color one often finds on trains in far-flung lands – the Indian woman with children and chickens all roaming the aisle; the teenage girl terrified of her first trip by rail; the rotund, small town entrepreneur, the only man on the train wearing a tie except for the conductor, regaling his fellow passengers with tales of his travels and commercial exploits, all the while excavating remnants of his lunch from his teeth by means of a gold toothpick, and so on. In other words, a typical mélange of passengers crossing the vast Brazilian back country.

The old wooden carriages had no air conditioning and all the windows were open, as we were, after all, well within the Tropic of Capricorn, and the air was hot and sultry. This had the drawback of admitting the occasional cloud of sooty black smoke from the old coal-burning engine, but moving air was more important than a little soot, so nobody complained.

After a while, the elderly conductor came through the car, calling, "*Janelas acima*," and everybody began dutifully closing the windows. The temperature outside must have been in the nineties, and I couldn't see the logic in the shutting out our only source of ventilation, but I put the window up anyway.

After maybe five minutes of rumbling along in the stifling car, I was muttering about being treated like a clam being steamed, but my thoughts were interrupted by the sound of objects striking the sides of the rail car and its windows. I looked out and saw what appeared to be sticks bouncing off the glass.

My unasked question was answered for me by the gold toothpick-wielding entrepreneur, who began expounding on how the government ought to dispatch the army out here and clear all these damned Indians out of the area once and for all. It was a disgrace, he said, for people paying full fare for a railroad ticket to have arrows shot at them by a bunch of Indians. The other people on the train said nothing, just shrank back from the closed windows. As I happened to be speechless, I did likewise.

Now, that happened in South America, where other tales to follow happened. I also have memories of Asia, the South Pacific and other areas, but most of my traveling during the decade beginning in 1955 was in Europe – West and East, including the USSR. I have not set down the year of each tale, as I think that would become tiresome. Just remember that everything mentioned in this book took place in that late '50s-early '60s period.

All my life since the age of sixteen I have done a lot of traveling, the majority of it involving groups which I have accompanied to all parts of the world as a tour operator for over half a century, but also on an independent basis, as I caught "the travel bug" early and am still afflicted with it. As a college-age kid I worked my way around South America, and I planted trees in Spain for the Franco government – more on that later.

Brazil: Welcome to the Mato Grosso

1

And How Cheap Was It?

STRETCHING ONE'S PENNIES A LONG WAY

I do not plan to dwell throughout this book on examples of how cheap things were at the time, so I will devote a little space here to doing just that. Then we will move on to more anecdotes and adventures.

As mentioned above, costs were low in most other countries primarily due to a recovery process since the ending of World War II in 1945. This was particularly true in the countries of the two big losers, Germany and Japan. And Spain; but that is another story to be discussed further on. In recent years, the U.S. dollar rate has dropped as low as 80 Japanese yen to the dollar, but during the time of this book, one got 360 yen to the dollar, and that was without the Japanese government lopping off zeros from their currency, as the French did at the time.

In Rio de Janeiro, at the great jewelry firm of Stern's, I bought my mother some amethyst and gold earrings for $7.00 U.S. Recently I went to Stern's in Rio (bearing my original sales receipt) and found the same earrings, now priced at $3,500.00 U.S.

There were two big books for American travelers to Europe in those days, one for Darby and Jill who live on the hill, and one for the penny-pinching set (which included me, when I was not leading a group trip). Darby owned the Studebaker dealership in Podunk, Georgia, while Jill headed up the Junior League. Their travel guidebook was an annual publication by the American travel guru Temple Fielding, who would direct readers to the finest hotels in the main tourist cities, such as the Negresco in Nice, where one might pay the rather large sum of $7.70 for a double room, and $4.00 for a dinner at Tour d' Argent in Paris.

The penny-pinchers, on the other hand, relied on Arthur Frommer's new *Europe on $5 a Day*. This book revealed the really cheap hotels, pensiones and eateries, and was the virtual Bible of many American travelers on a shoestring budget. This lot included teachers, social workers, young unmarrieds on leave from the office, and, of course, students. I had no problem staying within the $5 a day limit per the book. But, as related in a story further on, at least one European student was horrified upon reading the book's title, and he shouted to me that only rich Americans could afford to spend so much.

The U.S. dollar was accepted everywhere in the world, including of course, Europe, which reminds me of a story which does not really belong in this chronicle, as it occurred later, in the 1970s, I think it was. But I'll tell it, nevertheless. Anyway, the U.S. dollar had undergone a drastic blow *vis-à-vis* European currencies (pre-euro), and its worth had (temporarily) dropped considerably. The story is that an elderly blind Frenchman with a white cane and wearing dark glasses is standing on the Champs-Elysées in Paris, his beret lying bottom-up at his feet, with a few coins dropped into it by passers-by. An American tourist sees him, pulls out his wallet, and extracts a dollar bill. The blind man raises his hand in the "Stop!" position and says, in English, "No dollars!"

Well, dollars or francs or pesetas or whatever, it was all still money, and while I found everything to be quite inexpensive in Europe, I was still stunned at seeing people *buying* water at sidewalk cafes. I had never heard of bottled water, mineral or otherwise, and I couldn't believe it. I tasted it, and it was just water. Same as you got out of the tap. Unbelieveable. And in some places, a glass of table wine from the barrel was cheaper than bottled water. Insane!

That wine from the barrel could be had for a dime per full bottle in Spain. You could sip it while you got a three-cent shoeshine.

But Spain wasn't the only bargain place. In London one could find a nice room in any one of dozens of B-and-Bs for a pound a night ($2.80 U.S.), including a full English breakfast of eggs, sausages, rolls or toast, coffee or tea, and (canned) orange juice. Bernard Street, just off Russell Square, was shoulder to shoulder with such places. They are all long gone now, victims of the wrecking ball.

Yes, your pennies went a long way in England. And those pennies were BIG – as big as a U.S. half dollar. They came in handy for small purchases like postage stamps and calls from a red telephone box.

A two hour and twenty minute sightseeing tour of London in a red, double-decker bus set one back a whopping 56 cents.

Most Americans had a hard time understanding the British monetary system. Most currencies involved two units – like dollars and cents or marks and pfennigs – or even only one unit, as with Italian lire, Spanish pesetas, etc. But a pound sterling, worth $2.80 U.S., was broken down further into two more units: 20 shillings, each worth 14 cents U.S., and each shilling divided into 12 pence. Thus an item's price of two pounds, ten shillings and 6 pence was written thusly: £2/10-/6d. And, to further complicate matters, there were coins designated as a crown, half-crown, florin, sixpence, halfpenny (pronounced "hape-ny") and farthings (half a halfpenny). Not to mention the guinea, which was a pound plus a shilling, used in bills presented by doctors, lawyers and such. No wonder so many Americans were baffled by this system!

But if you just remembered that a pound was $2.80, you could get along, for many things (such as the B-and-Bs mentioned above) were priced at an even pound. Similarly, the top price for a London show, a live performance at one of the theatres in the Shaftesbury Avenue area, was one pound – although balcony seats as cheap as one crown (75 cents U.S.) were available. In lovely old grande dame theatres, small but with ornate and gilded side boxes and balconies, such as the Saville, Apollo, Her Majesty's and others, I saw such luminaries of the show world as John Gielgud, Ralph Richardson, Diana Wynyard, Peter Ustinov and Rex Harrison. And all live, for a few cents.

Now, Britain was cheap enough, but Germany and Austria were *really* cheap. Costs there were about a third of those in the U.K. A liter mug of beer at the famous Hofbrauhaus in Munich was one mark or 26 cents U.S., while in Innsbruck a complete dinner show of oompah and zither music and alpine yodeling and dancing at the renowned Stiftskeller was $1.50. More on this area later.

In Barcelona one evening, I departed from my usual practice of staying in modest pensiones and opted for a room in the finest five star deluxe hotel in town, the Ritz. The cost was one dollar, U.S. I still have the receipt.

Also in that same city, Barcelona, I met up with a couple of American student types who wanted to go on a Cook's night club tour. I wasn't much of one for tours, but I said okay and joined them. The cost was staggering, to me: $4.00 U.S. But looking back on it, it was cheap as hell. We went to three different flamenco clubs, with drinks included at each, and our arrival at each club was timed so that we entered just before the show was to begin. The flamenco dancing and singing was very good, I thought, but it soon became apparent that the señoritas dancing with the castanets were also proficient in other areas. After finishing their portion of the show – with other dancers taking over – some of the young ladies made their way to the banquette where I and my friends were sitting and began to, uh, get chummy. I got the message fast when a small hand, hidden beneath the voluminous folds of a polka-dotted flamenco skirt which flowed over my lap, suddenly latched onto, er, *me*. I gathered she was asking me for a date. My friends were likewise appealed to. But we had already paid a huge sum for the tour, and enough was enough. We bade the ladies *adios*.

On a different occasion in Barcelona, I was with an American friend I had met, and as he had a youth hostel card and wanted to use it, I said okay and we went to the local hostel. The place was not conveniently located – it was to the north of the city center, in the Tibidabo district, occupying a big house which appeared to have been an impressive mansion in some bygone time, but which now looked like a well-trashed fraternity house on its last legs. We went through some ornate old gates and up a path through some ruined gardens, to a crude desk set up inside the front door. I didn't like the looks of the place: it reminded me of movies I had seen, where the recently victorious Bolsheviks had taken over a nice bourgeois house and turned it into a pig sty housing many turnip farmer families from the steppes. But I went ahead and paid the 20 pesetas (30 cents U.S.) charge for an overnight, only to learn later that our beds were cotton bags stuffed with wood shavings and located in a big room with some eight other beds, the occupants of which clomped around all night, smoking, and never shut up. To make matters worse, the next morning the commissar or whatever the student-boss was called – a jerk of a Dutchman – thrust a broom into my hand and told me to sweep up the plentiful leakings of wood shavings strewn about this and other rooms. That did not sit well with me; I had paid 20 pesetas for a bed, not to join a work brigade. I told the commissar what he could do with his broom, and he shouted at me to get out; I would not be welcome there any more. In a sort of "You can't fire me – I quit!" retort, I grabbed my small bag and exited the place forever, with no hope of ever returning. My bridges were burned.

Speaking of my small bag, which was a cheap nylon suitcase maybe 24"x18"x8", all Americans, even the lowliest student types (like me, before my work with groups) carried suitcases. This was before the Backpack Era came in – for U.S. travelers, that is. European students, especially Germans, were already blazing the way with their rucksacks. Real *Walderee-Waldera* specimins, each usually with a long loaf of bread, maybe a salami-like sausage and a bottle of water protruding from his (or her) pack.

And on the subject of food, French chow was tops then, just as it is now. I found a little restaurant in Montmartre where, for $1.30 U.S., I could get eggs mayonnaise, a nice steak (entrecote), potatoes, bread, a half liter of wine and chocolate mousse, all absolutely delicious.

And later in the evening, you could go to the famed Lido for what was very possibly the most spectacular show in the world; if you watched from the bar and nursed a single drink the whole time, your total tab was $2.85 U.S.

But I confess I did get ripped off on my first visit to Paris. I made a mistake and ordered a Coca-Cola at a bar on the posh Rue de Rívoli. When the bartender popped the cap and announced that the price was 200 francs, or 40 cents U.S., I almost choked. The most I had ever paid for a Coke was a dime, and most places in the U.S. the price was a nickel. But the guy had already opened the bottle, so there was nothing left but to fork over the 200 francs. (Shortly thereafter, as I think I mentioned, the French government lopped off the last two zeroes from their currency, in order to make it look more like the money of their northern neighbors.

Italy never did this zero-lopping business. The Eyeties just stayed with the multi-zeroed lire, 600 of them to the dollar. A common bill in use was the 10,000 lire note, worth $16.00 U.S. and so big – about 4 x 8 inches – that you had to fold it twice to get it to fit in your wallet. For a couple of hundred of dollars' worth of these huge bills, one could have wallpapered his bathroom.

Occasionally one could, admittedly, run into some pretty stiffly priced hotels. My first time in Venice, I had a very difficult time finding a place to stay, and when I finally did, the medium-level hotel (the Bonvecchiati – a nice place, actually) charged me $3.80 U.S. for a room. Thought I was going to die. Half a century later, that same standard room went for $400.00 U.S.

When I first went to Europe, I had never seen a soccer game, and I finally got my chance in Switzerland. I saw the Zurich Grasshoppers beat the team from Chiasso, 9-1. My ticket to the stands (literally – a slope for standing only, no seats) cost me 70 cents U.S. The Swiss fans cheered enthusiastically but remained properly restrained – unlike the fans at my second soccer match.

This second one took place a year later in Montevideo, Uruguay, and pitted the local team, from the metro area called Cerro, against a team from someplace I'd never heard of. Once again I was in the seatless stands, from where I watched the local team fall behind the visitors, enraging the spectators. Now, I had already noted that the teams and the referees entered and exited the field via tunnels opening into the sidelines via holes in the ground, and that between the field and the stands there was a deep, waterless concrete moat behind a fierce-looking barbed wire fence. And a good thing, too, because when the final whistle sounded and the Cerro team had lost, the crowd was a *manicomio* (madhouse) screaming invectives at the game's officials, who were of course responsible for the visitors' undeserved victory. People threw themselves onto the barbed wire fence, yelling and shaking their fists, while the players of both teams and the referees made for the tunnels asap. Some local fan with good aim launched an empty liter grappa bottle at a ref, catching the poor man in the side of his head, felling him instantly. The police went wild, swinging their billy clubs at anybody and everybody. I ducked my head and, mercifully, escaped unscathed. I think I had paid about 20 cents U.S. to attend this lively event.

But enough about what things cost. Time to move on to actual travel experiences in the bargain world.

2

An American in Paris
- and Elsewhere

FAIR BRUSSELS

In 1935 there was a world's fair in Brussels, and in 1939 one in New York. Then World War II came along and spoiled plans for one in Japan in 1940 and another in Rome in 1942. The first postwar world's fair was held once again in Brussels in 1958, and it was quite a show. (The fair's centerpiece, the 335-foot-tall Atomium, still remains today as a testament to that great exposition.) I took in the fair, spending two or three days going through the various nations' exhibits. Not surprisingly, the two most-visited sites were those of the United States and the Soviet Union. The U.S. pavilion featured for the most part items of modern American life: cars, washing machines, TV sets (including an early color model), etc. The Soviets focused on factories, tractors and murals of happy, toothless workers joining hands and charging through the turnip fields.

One of the most interesting sights to me was that of a couple of big, platinum blonde Scandinavian girls (twins?), Jayne Mansfield types, wearing tight sky-blue sweaters and short skirts, and probably measuring 50-20-36. They were ubiquitous at the fair, turning up everywhere one went, always flanking a different, grinning sucker who would be "in" until his money was gone; then he would be replaced by yet another grinning fool. Watching these two amazons being squired around the fair became a popular pastime of the attendees, myself included. Later I found one of the aforementioned male escorts sitting alone on a park bench; he was bent over, his elbows on his knees and he was shaking his head.

Downtown Brussels was like most cities in Europe: the buildings were all sooty black from the smoke of soft coal fires and belching factory chimneys. At the end of the day the inside of your shirt collar would be similarly black, requiring regular washing in the sink in your hotel room, if you had one, or otherwise (and most likely) in the floor's one bathroom at the end of the hall. This was the era of the much-heralded, all-nylon wash-n-wear clothing. One looks back on such clothing – shirts, pants, underwear, everything – with great distaste, but it was good for one thing, and that was do-it-yourself washing, as clothes would be dry and ready to go again in no time.

Those black building façades, by the way, were to undergo a Europe-wide sandblasting cleaning job later in the sixties, revealing cream-colored faces. But all that was still to come.

By the way, the cities' chimneys were not the only source of smoke. All the *people* smoked as well. And I mean *everybody*. I swear that, especially in the countries bordering the Mediterranean, even five-year-old kids smoked. Americans were no exception; it seemed to me they all smoked, as well. I was never a smoker, but believe me, I was in the vast minority. It is a fact that I knew *nobody* – zero, zilch – who didn't smoke.

And Europe was chock full of those smoking Americans. They were everywhere, especially in the top hotels. I can remember the lobby of the five star Palace Hotel in Lucerne filled to overflowing with U.S. tourists, all smoking and jabbering away over their *Fielding's Travel Guides* (no *Europe on $5 a Day* copies amongst *that* lot, I assure you). But the last time I was in that same lobby, not long ago, I was the only American present. That's what happens when the cost of a hotel room soars to a hundred times the old price in a person's lifetime.

SHOES IN THE NIGHT

At night, the room doors in the hallways of better hotels were usually fronted by pairs of shoes waiting to be shined by a hotel employee during the night. In the morning, the shoes would be back, all shiny. Some hotels had little "shoe doors" down beside the room door, sort of like those dog/cat doors some homes have. The newly shined shoes would be placed inside the guest room foyer via one of these little doors. No tipping was involved here, as you never knew who actually shined the shoes. I remember one time seeing a tiny red pair of children's shoes patiently waiting outside a room door – no adult shoes accompanying them. Maybe the kid was there on single room basis.

THE IDIOT BOX ARRIVES IN EUROPE

I can recall seeing one television set in a European hotel lobby. It was in a side parlor of the (now long gone) Hotel France et Choiseul on the Rue St. Honoré in Paris, and apparently somewhat of a novelty, as quite a few people were staring slackjawed at the small black and white picture. I even remember what was showing: it was a Glenn Ford western, *The Sheepman*, with a dubbed-in French soundtrack. It was humorous to me to see Ford the cowboy draw his sixgun and snarl, *Arret, m'sieu! Je sois le gran fou Tex de Tombstone!* Or something like that.

I don't remember ever seeing a TV set in Spain in the early days, however, not even in an appliance store window. Maybe Franco had one, and he could watch endless reruns of an old biographical film about himself, with special emphasis on his heroic role in the Spanish Civil War, which had ended 19 or 20 years earlier.

LE GRAND CHARLES TO THE RESCUE

And speaking of civil war, the newspapers and radio screamed that France was on the verge of it in 1958. That country was seriously divided at the time over the issue of Algeria, then still a possession of France. Leftists wanted to grant the big colony independence and thus bring to an end the ongoing terrorism by Algerian muslims inside France, while the Rightists, including much of the military, wanted to keep the status quo. Supporters of the latter group made themselves known by driving through the streets honking on their car horns in a *Honk-honk-honk, honk! Honk!* pattern, meaning, *Al-ger-ie Fran-çaise!* I was of course seriously concerned that all this bickering was going to spoil my time in France. After all, it's just no good trying to enjoy an aperitif in a sidewalk café if bullets and bombs are flying about. Then, like a white knight on his mighty steed, General Charles de Gaulle, he of World War II fame, charged onto the scene, took over, and shut everybody up. Paris and la Belle France were saved for the loyal readers of *Fielding's Travel Guide to Europe*

DOWN AND OUT IN PARIS

Now I will relate a happening which negates the "dirt cheap" appellation for my early days in Europe. This was most definitely an aberration; I experienced it one evening in Paris when I would have welcomed a street demonstration out of control – or anything to draw attention away from me long enough to make an escape. I refer to an instance in which things were *not* cheap for me. I had met two American students from North Carolina State University at the Louvre, and then the three of us had met, purely by chance, three American college girls, and we made a date to all go out to a night club later in the evening. The girls were from Kansas City but went to school at Wellesley; they were traveling with their parents on an escorted tour, and they had some sort of special dinner planned for tonight, which they felt duty bound to attend. Thus the after-dinner nightclub idea. So we met the girls in the lobby of their hotel, the Meurice, at nine o'clock or so, and we all piled into a taxicab (yes, all six of us), Montmartre bound. And we did the stupidest thing a foreign visitor to a European capital – especially Paris – could possibly do: we asked the taxi driver what was "a good nightclub in Montmartre." I suppose I should have suspected something when the cabbie smiled a huge, wicked, ear to ear smile like that evil Cheshire cat in the *Cinderella* cartoon movie and roared off for Paris's nighttime wonderland.

We were deposited at the door of a nightclub whose name I do not recall but which looked upon entering like a bordello of *premiere classe.* Everything was in red velvet. And we were the only people there. The maitre d' sported a Slick Larry pencil-thin mustache and long sideburns, an evening coat with long tails, and a grin even bigger than the cab driver's. He hurriedly conjured up six dainty chairs of the type my great aunt was so fond of, and placed them around a tiny, round table. And before one could say Jacques Robinson, a bucket of unordered champagne was there in its own stand – to be followed by more and more bottles of the bubbly. Almost immediately, a string trio of musicians, a cellist and two violinists, pulled up chairs around us and began playing *Rachmaninoff's Second Piano Concerto* (without a piano) – over and over. Man! Was this the life! The champagne kept coming, and we kept laughing and talking and guzzling. Six bottles of bubbly appeared – or was it eight? And *Rachmaninoff's Second Piano Concerto* was surely into its 200th rendition by now.

At last the girls said they had to get back to their hotel, lest their parents start worrying. I mentioned *Cinderella* earlier. Well, this was where the clock chimed midnight and our coach turned into a pumpkin: they brought the bill. The other two guys and I studied the piece of paper uncomprehendingly. Frankly, I don't remember the total due – probably because my mind simply blotted it all out, as sometimes happens when one is in a horrible carwreck or is seriously wounded in battle. It may have been $50.00, it may have been $50,000.00, it really didn't matter, because even amongst the three of us guys, there was *no way on earth* we could pay that bill. *And* we had to tip Rachmaninoff's boys. Fortunately, the girls – all from wealthy families and, thank God, with great wads of cash filling their petite, beaded evening bags – quickly ascertained our dilemma and bailed us out. We were mortified, as we couldn't possibly repay the money. Ever. Mercifully, our dates took it all in good stride. But what would have happened if ...? *Aiiiiiieeeee!* I don't even like to think about it! I must admit: This was a rare exception to the Dirt Cheap World.

On a different occasion in Paris, with two other American guys and two girls we'd met, we all agreed to go along with the suggestion of one of the girls, a music student at Julliard. She was a jazz fiend and wanted to go to a club called the Blue Note, which she said was famous. Me, at that time of my life, I didn't know progressive jazz from Dixieland, but I went along with the others, to what proved to be a sort of dark, smoky, hole-in-the-wall place run by a hefty American. On the bill for the night we visited was the American jazz clarinetist Zoot Sims, of whom I had never heard at the time. Being young college kids from the U.S. heartland, we arrived early, about 9:00 p.m. The place was empty. But a warm-up act was on the small stage: four French kids wearing James Dean duds and sporting Elvis-style ducktail hairdos. They were lounging about on some Folding chairs, smoking, their electric guitars and drums at the ready. When the owner seated the five of us at a table near the stage, the musicians all quickly scrambled to their feet and, after the usual thumping of and blowing into the microphone on a stand, they began a frantic rendition of Elvis's *Hound Dog*, in English. Or a sort of English:

You ain't nozzin boot a 'oun' dohg,
Juzza cryin' all ze tahm . . .

It was hilarious. The boys swiveled their hips outrageously as they sang and played, just as Ed Sullivan had feared Elvis would do when he appears on his *Talk of the Town* television show, prompting old Ed to order the cameramen to show Elvis from the waist up only. Later, the Blue Note's main attraction came on, and Zoot was good. But after all this time, what I remember most about that night is those French kids with their American-style ducktail haircuts singing in atrociously accented, Elvis-style, French-English.

You ain't nozzing boot a 'oun' dohg . . .

BACK AMONGST THE UPPER CRUST

At still a different time I ended up being invited to dinner at Maxim's in Paris by yet another set of American college girls traveling with their parents. I donned my one coat-and-tie outfit and joined the beautiful people at what was generally considered to be the finest restaurant in la Belle France. It was great, and at its end I happened to see the bill presented to one of the girls' fathers. The total was 80,000 francs, and as there were eight of us, that worked out to $50.00 U.S. per person. Fifty or sixty years later, the equivalent price would be about $750.00 a head. Now, *that* is eating high on the hog.

Contrast the above story with dinner in a Greek country restaurant of the time, where there was no menu, you just walked back into the steamy kitchen and peered into any number of big pots and bins of bubbling-hot stews, meats, casseroles, etc., and made your selections by simply pointing at the kettles with the food you wanted. All of which came with a small carafe of retsina wine and set you back a grand total of maybe 50 cents U.S.

But topping Maxim's, Zoot Zims, the French Elvis wannabees and even the Rachmaninoff string ensemble was an evening at the open-air theater situated within the ancient Baths of Caracalla in Rome, where a lavish production of Verdi's *Aida* was being staged. I regret to say that I cannot remember who sang the parts of Aida, Radames or Ramfis, but what I can never forget is the incredible procession of live animals which were part of the troupe. In addition to the cast of 300 singers and extras, there were elephants, camels, horses, donkeys and even a couple of pythons dangling from the necks of extras. The fact that we were outside of course made all the difference. That and the fact that it just cost two dollars. And as far as my opera-attending life has gone since then, it has all been downhill.

SHOES THAT WALKED WHERE JESUS WALKED

Big time tourism to "The Holy Land," generally meaning Israel, used to be a flourishing business primarily involving Christian church groups from the U.S., promoted to local congregations by individual ministers who were taught how to do it by large tour companies specializing in that sort of travel. The reward, of course, was one free trip – or the cash value thereof – for the minister, for each fifteen, or ten, or whatever number of paying participants on which the scheme was based. Obviously, the smaller the number of persons on which the "free" trips were prorated, the higher the selling price for the suckers who paid. The worst I ever heard of was one free trip for each two paying. People buying that tour were getting soaked, paying about fifty per cent over the trip's actual cost.

In retrospect, the roundtrip inclusive tour price of $499 from New York sounds cheap enough, especially when compared with the present day cost of perhaps $5,000 for a similar two-week tour. I shudder at the thought of what the markup would be on a modern-day "preacher tour."

The unfortunate upsurge of violence in the area in recent decades has put a damper on this business, but prior to the 1967 war it was huge. The following anecdote took place in the ancient coastal city of Caesarea. I have never found the Israelis to be too big on Roman remains, much preferring to reserve their admiration for things more closely tied to ancient Judea and Samaria and modern Israel. Still, it could be arranged for a group visiting that small nation to stop at a Roman site. On one particular occasion, my group visited Caesarea, on the coast between Tel Aviv and Haifa.

My participants had heard the guide's spiel and were now providing custom to the souvenir shops and dispensaries of food and drink in the little commercial center just off the beach. As I fully appreciated the uncontested fact that a large ration of dry information about the ancient Romans is best followed by an ingestion of twelve cold ounces of the local Maccabee beer at fifteen cents U.S., I left my charges to such pursuits and wandered over to the remains of an aqueduct which dated back to the days when Caesarea was the capital of Roman Palestine. The stone structure, thirty feet or so high, ended abruptly at mid-beach, leading to the obvious deduction that the coastline had receded over the centuries, since the now-broken-off aqueduct's end would now have been somewhere out to sea. After all, the water from the hills to the east was meant to end up in the city named for Caesar, not in the Mediterranean.

Standing in the shadow of the great ruin was a man who, from his appearance, I thought had to be an American. He turned and looked at me, then stepped in my direction, a big smile on his rather homely face and his right hand extended in a friendly, even eager greeting. Though on the beach, he wore a white shortsleeved business shirt, without tie, black trousers and black leather, lace-up dress shoes. He also wore a large pair of clear bifocal glasses, and he sported a modern ducktail hairdo with surging pompadour and longish sideburns, Elvis style. His black hair was well pomaded with yak butter.

"How do you do, sir?" he said cheerily. I supposed I had no option, so I shook his hand and murmured something.

"My name is Luke Bellows," he said, still pumping my hand and quite obviously assuming I spoke English. "Reverend Luke Bellows, actually. I'm a man o' God! Yes, sir."

Discreetly as I could, I glanced around, wondering if I should try to make a run for it. But I couldn't, as Reverend Bellows still had hold of my hand and was still pumping it. Finally he let go, but he plunged ahead verbally without any pauses, telling me that he came from Alabama, where he was the minister of a Baptist church in a small town. He began extolling the many magnanimous deeds performed by his church for its congregation and the community at large, but then he must have noticed my frantic glances to each side, with escape foremost in my mind, because he abruptly switched the topic.

Reverend Bellows pointed to his shoes, a pair of black, economy jobs, now rather sandy from walking on the beach.

"See these here shoes?" he said. "These shoes have walked where Jesus walked!" And before I could say anything, the reverend added, "Oh yes! Right up the Via Dolorosa, right to Golgotha, right to the real tomb of Jesus – not to the phony one the Church of Rome tries to pass off onto folks. Sorry, no offense if you're a Catholic, but that's just the truth and I know that down deep, you know it is, too."

I cleared my throat but said nothing.

Reverend Bellows continued. "Now, y'know, it's a sad fact that most of my congregation ain't never gonna git to come to the Holy Land. I been blessed – real blessed – in that regard. I git to travel free with church groups I git up, dontcha know? In fact, this here is my third trip to the Holy Land." He paused to let that stunning bit of information sink in, and I began muttering departure preparations, but my breakout efforts were futile, for Reverend Bellows seized my arm.

"How much do you think it can mean to a person who's never walked where Jesus walked – and who ain't *never* gonna walk where Jesus walked – to own a pair of shoes that've walked where Jesus walked?"

"I don't think I understand," I said.

"I mean, if you've got a pair of shoes that've walked where Our Lord walked, even if you yerself ain't, you can hold 'em, touch 'em, feel 'em, love 'em, caintcha? Heck, if they're the right size you could even *wear* 'em! They *mean* something to ya. Who knows? Maybe some old dried skin from Jesus's feet is stuck to the bottom of 'em!"

Reverend Bellows cast glances over his shoulders like a furtive peddler. "You know what? I got ten more pairs of shoes just like these, back in my room at the hotel. (He pronounced it *ho*-tel.) And ever' one of 'em has walked where Jesus walked. See, ever' time I come here, I take a whole bunch o' shoes in a big shopping bag to the Via Dolorosa, and I walk maybe half a block up and back in each pair! Then I take 'em back to Alabama and sell 'em to members of my congregation for a hunnerd dollars a pair! And I got 'em on sale for eight dollars at that new K-Mart in Birmingham!" He then chortled but apparently decided he had better clarify things.

"Look, I ain't trying to make money off my people, you know that. But I gotta cover my expenses, ain't I? And believe me, them poor souls who git a pair of these shoes that've walked where Jesus walked, well, it's sure worth it to them!"

"Yes, well, how do you suppose the Romans had the engineering knowhow to construct something like this aqueduct?" I said. I had to change the subject.

Reverend Bellows adapted surprisingly well. The shoes saga apparently left behind, he seized upon the new topic.

"Well, as I figger it," he said, "the Romans needed a lot of this here sea water up there in them hills. It's bone dry up there, you know. Grow crops and all, I s'pose."

"But sea water is salt water," I said.

"Yeah, that's true. I s'pose the Romans figgered out some way to git the salt out of it. What'd be the point of sending all that sea water up into them hills otherwise?"

"But to send water from sea level up into those hills defies the law of gravity."

Reverend Bellows looked up into the dry Samarian hills, squinting in the bright sunlight.

"Yeah, them Romans was crafty fellers, all right," he said, now pausing to bend down and dust off with a handkerchief his shoes which had walked where Jesus walked. "A pretty slick bunch, if you ask me."

Israel: The man in the shoes that walked where Jesus walked

3

Britain:
I Say, Jolly Good Show!

IT'S SHOWTIME!

One of the best things about going to London was being able to see some of the best theatre in the world, for incredibly low prices, even for the time. As I mentioned earlier, one could go to any performance of the legitimate theatre for the *maximum* price of one pound ($2.80 U.S.), and if you sat in the balcony as I did, the price could be as low as 75 cents U.S.

An English friend, a fellow named David whom I had known in college, took me to see a highly popular comedy team, Flanders and Swan, in a performance at the Fortune Theatre called *At the Drop of a Hat*. It was a two-man production without any stage props except a piano, but those two kept the audience entertained nonstop with song ditties parodying current events. One song, called *In the Bath*, had Ike and Khruschev resolving the world's problems while in a big, suds-filled bathtub.

I became very fond of the farces of funnyman Brian Rix. I saw many of his shows, such as *One for the Pot*, and all were hilarious. Rix practically owned the Garrick Theatre.

Political correctness had not yet reached the shores of Fair Albion, as witnessed by the title of a popular Agatha Christie mystery on the stage, *Ten Little Niggers*. The title was changed for its run on Broadway to *Ten Little Indians*.

Many Americans, including myself, as well as other foreigners, got caught with our pants down, so to speak, the first time I and they attended a live theatre performance in London. When the final curtain came down at the end of that first show, I instinctively slipped quickly out of my seat and into the aisle, in an effort to beat at least part of the crowd to the exit. Happily, most of the audience seemed in no hurry to leave. I had taken perhaps four or five steps up the aisle when the orchestra began booming out *God Save the Queen*. I lurched to a stop and turned around. Everyone was standing, virtually at attention, as the majestic anthem played. Along with a handful of other aliens, I stood there frozen, like Lot's wife – and embarrassed as hell. At least the theatre lighting was still low; hopefully, my red face wouldn't be all that obvious. I had learned the hard way to stay at my seat after the final curtain at future performances, until the queen's salute had been played. The ritual post-performance playing of *God Save the Queen* was dropped a few years later at all theatres.

One day I happened to be walking in the area of St. Paul's Cathedral, and I noticed something going on out front of the great church. It seemed that a movie was being shot, and a chalked sign on a board told me that it was *Lawrence of Arabia*. The scene being filmed had a large crowd of dressed-up men in top hats and ladies in frumpy dresses descending the wide front staircase. In the forefront was one of my favorite actors, Jack Hawkins, and he was intercepted in his descent by a reporter type who rushed up to him, pencil and notepad in hand, and began speaking to him. Then the director cried, "Cut!" and everybody remounted the steps, to shoot the scene again. After three or four takes, I went on my way. I saw the film later and immediately recognized the scene, which followed T. E. Lawrence's funeral service at St. Paul's.

A fabulous place, now long gone, was located right at Piccadilly Circus: the Trocadero, a 1000-room hotel with a dining room which was, to me, like something out of the Arabian Nights. It was a huge place, decorated like a sultan's palace and with large potted palms all about. An orchestra played as the patrons dined and danced, with turban-wearing African waiters doing the serving. I was taken there by my friend David, and the place blew my mind. Many years later another establishment, also called the Trocadero, was built there, but it was (and is) nothing compared with the original.

Before I arrived in London for the first time, my friend David told his father I was a friend of his and was coming to London and then, after that, up to Yorkshire to visit him. His father very graciously made London hotel reservations for me – prepaid, at that – and did the same for me at a hotel near to where they lived in the north. I can tell you, all this was most appreciated by me.

The celebrated London hotel in question, unknown to most Americans, was a quaint old place on Jermyn Street called the Cavendish Hotel (not to be confused with the present-day Cavendish, built in the 1970s). I did not at the time realize what a treat was in store for me.

When I subsequently arrived at the hotel in London, I found myself in what seemed to be an old Victorian house, despite its location just off Piccadilly Circus. The lobby was like a living room, and there was no registration desk per se: an antique secretary served that purpose. In the center of the room was what appeared to be a dining room table, and it was covered with recently arrived mail for the guests, all neatly divided into individual stacks. One just went to the table and sought out his mail, if there was any for him.

There was no lift, so there were stairs to climb to the floors above with the guest rooms, and once in your antique-filled room, you were advised by the venerable old gentleman in tails who had shown you up that there were no room keys. "Our guests do not steal," he explained, sniffing the air. Asked about checkout, the same antediluvian chap replied, "Our guests do not *check out.* They *leave.*"

It turned out that this hotel had been the longtime home of Rosa Lewis, many years later portrayed in the British television series, *The Duchess of Duke Street.* Miss Lewis had, in the 19th century, been a famous courtesan and, later, the full-time "friend" of King George V. She had died fairly recently, but her establishment was still going. In the '60s the building was demolished to make way for a much taller structure on this prime real estate.

After London I took the train to Yorkshire and visited my friend David. While I was there, another American college friend of David's "popped in" for a visit, a short, 19-year-old North Carolinian with a buzz cut, named Gene. He was a very laid-back fellow who chewed gum constantly and who did not seem to be impressed by anything. On a beautiful Sunday in summer, David's father and mother invited all of us to go on a Sunday afternoon drive, apparently as popular a notion in England as it was in the U.S. at the time. We all said yes, sure, and soon we were driving through the bucolic countryside on a sunny day, in the family car, a big Lagonda. Although the car was new, it – like all British cars of the time – looked like an American car from the late 1930s. It was black, of course, with leather upholstery, and it smelled good, as new cars do.

We visited the remains of an old abbey, where cows wandered through and around the old structure, and then we drove on to a town named Middleham. There the main attraction was what was left of an ancient castle, the ruined walls and towers poking up into the sky. The laconic Gene studied the scene for a minute or so, slowly chewing away at his gum, then drawled, "Looks like Middleham lost."

England: "Looks like Middleham lost."

4

Achtung! Travels in West Germany and Austria

POKING THROUGH THE RUINS

It will come as no surprise to read that of all the countries of Western Europe, Germany retained the most ruins from the war. British and American bombing raids virtually every day for years, sometimes involving a thousand planes or more, did a hell of a job on German cities – payback for the earlier, massive Luftwaffe bombing missions over London and other metropolitan areas. Berlin was the worst hit; as mentioned earlier, except for some main streets, East Berlin still looked like a ruined city. Even in West Berlin, fifty percent of the city was in ruins: hollow, bombed-out buildings and rubble-filled vacant lots.

Poking around in some ruins in the formerly elegant district of West Berlin just to the north of the great central park, the Tiergarten, I found some pieces of a fairly large, glazed tile plaque with blue letters on white which, when pieced together, read, *British Consulate*.

All major German cities had their share of war ruins, while many little villages were the same storybook-looking places they had always been. After Germany, I would have to say that northern Italy, and especially Milan, seemed to have suffered the worst damage. But even London still had its share of ruins and "bomb sites," now empty lots.

Especially in Bavaria and Austria, and particularly among the elderly, many people still wore the traditional dress: dirndls and puffy-sleeved blouses for women and *lederhosen* with knee socks and alpine hats with tiny feathers for men. I of course just dressed like an American and, especially in the earliest years, I was very often taken for one of the thousands of U.S. soldiers stationed in Germany, wearing "civvies" (my real army duty came later). A lot of Germans had seen enough of American army occupation forces, and if I asked a question, in German or in English, they would often pretend not to understand. Just as many Parisians like to pretend they can't understand the French of Americans or even the French of Quebec.

DER MEISTERSINGER

At the Hofbrauhaus in Munich on one occasion, I was sitting in an open air courtyard area with two American soldiers in "civvies", drinking those big liter steins of the house beer, priced at one Deutschmark, or twenty-six cents U.S. An old stone fountain bubbled happily next to our table. Hefty German waitresses carrying four huge steins in each hand delivered beer to the tables. We could not help but notice nearby a big, blond Bavarian man dressed in the traditional costume of *lederhosen* and knee socks, who was singing mightily, hoisting his stein of beer skyward as he did so. Other patrons were laughing and raising their own steins to him as he sang. About this time I announced to my new friends that I was going to take a bathroom break, and I left the table.

When I came back, the big blond man was sitting at our table, bellowing his song and waving his stein around in the air. My two friends were laughing and egging him on. I sat down in the remaining chair, as the man finished his song and began quaffing from his liter stein which, like all the steins in service, did indeed look as though it were made of stone (*stein*), although the mugs were actually of gray-colored ceramic.

The Bavarian turned and looked at me with a big smile on his ruddy face, then cried, "*Ach! Der Meistersinger!*" One of my laughing friends allowed as how they had told the man that I was a *Meistersinger*, and now the guy was beating me on the back, demanding that I sing with him. I laughed and said no, no, I couldn't do that, but that *he* should sing for us.

"*Nein!*" the big Bavarian shouted in reply. He was now scowling. He had apparently already put away several of those liter beers. "*Singen Sie, Meistersinger!*" he shouted, standing up and yanking me to my feet by one arm. His grip was powerful. He was about fifty years old and looked as though he might have been an *Oberfeldwebel*, or master sergeant, in the *Wehrmacht* some fifteen years back. Anyway, he was now red in the face and *demanding* that I sing with him.

Well, as they say, discretion is often the better point of valor, and so I grabbed my stein and held it high with my free arm, as the Bavarian began singing an off-key version of some German operatic piece. He suddenly stopped and glared at me, as I wasn't singing. Hell, I didn't know the words! But that argument wouldn't fly with this big fellow.

"*Meistersinger! Singen Sie!*" he roared, still gripping my arm tightly. He then resumed his aria, watching me as I tentatively began "singing." Actually, I was simply opening my mouth and bellowing out sounds, trying to match the sounds the Bavarian was making. After a few bars, I had it going pretty good, blaring sounds like "Waaaa, blaaah, bababaaa!" etc. Now not only my two friends, but much of the terrace crowd were laughing and cheering our act.

When the song mercifully came to an end, the hulking Bavarian threw his now-empty stein at the large stone fountain to our side, shattering the ceramic jug into a million pieces. The crowd loved it and cheered. But our waitress was of another opinion. She stopped her serving and rushed to our table, her massive hands on her broad hips. Inside that frilly blouse and dirndl skirt was about 250 pounds of angry *Frau*. Her flaxen pigtails bounced as she shouted a string of invectives at the now-silenced Bavarian, shaking a meaty finger in his face. The man looked surprised and bent backward, trying to avoid the wagging finger, as the *Frau's* cussing-out continued. Finally the big fellow turned tail and ran, exiting the courtyard and disappearing into the gloom of the inner beerhall. The waitress, her hands now on her hips again, stared after him, then finally gave a satisfied, curt and quick nod, an acknowledgement of her victory. The crowd applauded.

And thus ended my brief career as *Der Meistersinger*.

VIENNA IS NOT ITALIA

In Vienna one time in my youthful days, I came across another young American looking for someone to share a room with, as was the prevailing custom with U.S. youths at large in Europe. We located a lady who had an inexpensive room to rent in her flat, and we moved in accordingly. One day we did some some long overdue washing of our grungy clothes, using the common bathroom on our floor, and we hung everything out to dry on the iron railing bordering our tiny balcony overlooking the busy street below. A little later, our landlady, Frau Hauser, came beating on our door. I opened it and she charged in like a maddened bull, heading straight for the balcony, where our clothes hung limply.

Furiously, she yanked all our still-damp items off the railing and piled them on a wooden chair. "Ziss iss not Italia!" she cried, then stormed out. We re-hung the clothes around our room on chairs, from drawers and from the simple chandelier.

Vienna: "Ziss iss not Italia!"

On a Saturday, Frau Hauser invited my friend, a Brooklynite named Bob, and me to go with her to the family garden on the outskirts of Vienna. Many European city dwellers have small plots located in areas with many other such garden sites, maybe fifty feet square, including a little shack for tools – and maybe even a cot for weekend overnights. It seemed that Frau Hauser's husband – a man we'd never met – was working in their garden this weekend, tending to tomato plants, cabbages, etc., and she was taking a packed lunch to him. We said why not and rode a bus with the *gnädige Frau* to the end of the line, then walked a half mile or so to the place.

Herr Hauser was a tall, very thin man of maybe fifty years, with a lot of gray in his dark hair. He had a sunken chest and didn't look too healthy to me. Earlier, his wife had told us that her husband, newly married, had fought with the Germans against the Red Army at Stalingrad, and had been taken prisoner by the Russians in 1943. He was kept in a prison camp in the Soviet Union for twelve years, long after the war was over, during which time all but 5,000 of the 90,000 prisoners taken had died, mostly from exposure to the sub-zero winter conditions in an open camp. Finally in 1955 the Soviets released the surviving ex-Wehrmacht soldiers, and Herr Hauser came home to his wife. They had no children. "He iss ein man zat iss broken," she had confided to us. To us, he was quite pleasant, if rather restrained. His gray eyes seemed very sad to me. We sat on folding chairs and poked around the garden while he ate his sandwich and drank his half bottle of wine, then we said *auf wiedersehen*, shook his hand and returned to Vienna.

While in Vienna, Bob and I saw posters announcing a performance of *Tosca* at the Stadtsoper coming up in a day or two, and we agreed that we would like to try to see it. The night of the opera, we went to the opera house and stood in line at the students' ticket window, and we lucked up. We got standing room only tickets for three schillings, or twenty cents U.S., apiece and enjoyed a wonderful evening. Renata Tebaldi was magnificent.

5

Eastern Europe: Speak into the Flowers, Please

MEETING BIG BROTHER

American travel to the Soviet Union and the "East Bloc" countries was not nearly as popular as that to Western Europe; still, there were always those inquisitive souls who wanted to see what it was like behind the Iron Curtain, the lair of the enemy. For the most part, these travelers were not your timid soul types. They tended to be better educated and more widely traveled.

I was in that part of the world more often than most, always for one of three reasons. In my earliest days it was just ordinary independent travel, then escorting tour groups, and eventually, traveling for the purpose of setting up travel programs with Eastern European and Soviet government tourism officials. The latter proved to be the most interesting to me.

The "Red scare" and the Cold War were still going strong. Senator Joe McCarthy's Unamerican Activities Committee days were over, but Soviet leader Nikita Khruschev was still banging his shoe on the podium at the United Nations and shouting "We will bury you!" We being the Soviets, and You being the U.S. And the Russians had launched their Sputnik, while our space rockets were still blowing up on their pads. As one stand-up TV comic said, "Our space program is like the Civil Service: You can't fire it, and you can't make it work."

Look, back home in the good old U. S. of A, weren't school children practicing the occasional atomic bomb attack drills, during which they hid under their old wooden desks when the sirens sounded? (Like being under a little desk was going to protect them!) And weren't people encouraged to join the Ground Observer Corps, with members taking time out each day to go to the rooftop and scan the skies with binoculars, on the lookout for A-bomb-carrying Ilyushin or Tupolev bombers?

So, perhaps understandably, most American tourists to Eastern Europe felt sure their hotel rooms were bugged, and that guy sitting over there, across the lobby reading a newspaper, was for sure watching them. And hadn't that particular man back there, fifty feet behind them on the sidewalk, been following them for some time?

People in groups I was escorting to this area were forever asking me, "Don't you think they bug our rooms? Go through our suitcases? Follow us through the streets?" My answer was always the same: "I suppose it's possible, but then they do have maybe a million foreign tourists a year. I really doubt that they have the manpower to snoop on each and every visitor." Well, that wasn't what they wanted to hear. All that spooky stuff was, well, sort of *fun*. I mean, the bad guys might be checking them out, but, after all, they *were* Americans, in an American tour group, so they were really pretty safe – weren't they? A running joke – or was it a joke? – was to say to the person you were talking to, "Speak into the flowers, please."

I must confess that there were a few episodes which indicated that the fears of American travelers as to Big Brother snooping were true, at least to some extent. I had a group finishing up a tour of the USSR in Leningrad. Two people in my flock, a Jewish couple from New York, had told me they had relatives living in the city, and they planned to visit them, to meet them for the first time. I told them that such a deviation from the tour program was supposed to be a no-no, but they were adamant, so I just shrugged. I had said my piece; I wasn't a policeman. Then I just forgot about it.

Eastern Europe: Speak into the flowers, please!

When the time came for us to fly out of Leningrad and the USSR on our last day there, we all went by bus to the airport and prepared to go through what I knew would probably be the usual grueling procedure. And it was. Passport control took a very long time, and then came Soviet customs. Now most countries do not have a customs check on travelers *leaving* -- just on arriving. But nothing was easy in the USSR, and everyone had to go through a rigorous baggage inspection, with the uniformed KGB agents in their green uniforms with sky-blue shoulder epaulettes brusquely ordering each person in turn to open his or her bags. I say rigorous, but I guess I should clarify that: rigorous by U.S. Customs standards: they poked through things, pulled out a couple of items, looked at them and roughly stuffed them back, then barked at the owners to close their bags and move on. But when came the turn of my Jewish couple from New York, Katy, bar the door! Those KGB agents ripped that couple's suitcases apart and, finally, tucked under the satin-looking lining of one bag, they found three letters in addressed but unstamped envelopes. The minions took the man and the woman into a back room.

I was of course worried sick, but there was nothing I could do. The relatives had asked my tour members to smuggle out the letters (to relatives in other countries) and then post them once they were outside the USSR and beyond the censor's reach. I of course had no idea what would happen to my unfortunate couple; if they weren't released by flight time, I would have no option but to board my group – and me with them, as we still had another stop in Helsinki after this. I would just have to telephone the American Consulate in Leningrad and see what could be done.

Mercifully, after having their letters confiscated and receiving a severe tongue-lashing from the KGB, the couple was released just in time for them to make our flight. Those two badly shaken New Yorkers were in tears, and they swore they would never, ever set foot in the Soviet Union again.

All the communist countries regulated tourism carefully. No just going there willy-nilly and "playing it by ear." One either went with an approved group with everything prearranged, or as an independent traveler with a fixed itinerary, a local guide and vouchers to cover all inclusions: transportation, hotels, meals, sightseeing, everything. All arrangements were made in advance through the state travel entity in each county. In the USSR it was Intourist; in Czechoslovakia, Cedok; in Hungary, Ibusz; in Poland, Orbis – and so on.

You could actually travel to all these countries without changing any U.S. dollars into the local currency. After all, there was nothing one would want to buy in the government-run stores – assuming there was anything at all on the store shelves. It was not uncommon to see a shop with nothing for sale.

One day I was in Moscow's most popular shopping street, called the Arbat. Suddenly a few people started running down a side street. Then others joined the race; soon dozens of people were racing down the street. I joined them, because I recognized this as a rush to someplace where – someone had heard – they were selling *something*. Anything. And I wanted to see what it was. We all ran down maybe a half block, then up some broad stairs and through a set of double doors, into a Russian-modern building. Once through the doors, the leaders of the pack turned right and raced down a long hallway. At the end was a shop – it looked like maybe a bakery shop – with two young attendants wearing white smocks standing behind an empty glass counter. Behind them were glass shelves, all totally devoid of anything. A man in front of the crowd asked the attendants something, and they just shook their heads. No. Nothing for sale. Just a rumor. The crowd slowly turned about and trudged back the way we had all come. False alarm.

MONEY IN THE EAST

Any money you did spend would almost assuredly be in one of the hard currency shops for foreigners (no locals allowed), where dollars, pounds, francs and other western currencies were accepted for the likes of American cigarettes, French perfume, Scotch whisky, etc., and some locally made items such as *matryoshka* (nesting) dolls or fur hats in Russia, Dresden figurines in East Germany, and so on. In other words, artsy-craftsy stuff – and a lot of junk. These state stores served a purpose for Westerners, for it was here that one could buy packs of Marlboros and cheap ballpoint pens, which could be used as tips; accepting actual cash money from a foreigner could end a local in the hoosegow.

If for any reason one did end up with some local currency, the difference was quickly obvious. East Bloc coins were mostly made of lightweight aluminum. Flip one into the air and call either "heads" or "tails" – it probably wouldn't matter, as chances are good the wind would have blown the coin away before it could hit the ground. Russian paper money was very small; it was not even as big as Monopoly money. And, in reality, worth about as much.

Westerners were discouraged from talking with the locals – if one knew enough Russian or Bulgarian or whatever to have a conversation – although German usually worked in Poland and Czechoslovakia. In the tourist hotels the staff spoke some English (probably not French, Italian, Spanish, etc.), but all those people were heavily indoctrinated and under constant observation and would not enter into a casual conversation.

In, say, twelve or fifteen years after the end of World War II, one could occasionally find an ordinary Russian who knew some German – often learned the hard way – and once in a while he or she would speak with me. One man did so, and it was obvious that he had fallen for the Party Line, hook, line and sinker. In German, discussing his lifestyle in the USSR, he sighed and said, "*Ja*, things are not so good here. But at least it is better than in America!"

EATING LIKE PARTY COMMISSARS IN BUDAPEST

Not too long after the failed Hungarian revolution, or counterrevolution, of 1956, before I was married, my brother Charles and I visited Budapest. Then, as now, the Magyar capital was a unique, eclectic collection of architectural styles: Gothic, Renaissance, Baroque and Romanesque, as well as spooky Transylvanian, almost- Byzantine, bizarre nineteenth century Hungarian Art Nouveau, Gaudí's early twentieth century Catalán modern (with balconies and rooflines drooping like butter carvings in the sun), and the brooding Germanic / Eastern European style I think of as Monstrous Vampire.

Newer styles, too, were in evidence, including Art Deco from the 1930s and the drab Russian modern of the 1950s. But regardless of the genre, everything seemed gray and virtually lifeless. The city was still bullet-pocked and showing the results of the futile uprising of the Hungarians against their Russian occupiers, and the people on the streets were shabbily dressed. Although given the chance, we would have chosen a more modest hotel, in order to get visas for

Hungary we had no alternative but to prepurchase vouchers good for a nice hotel (still very inexpensive) and all the restaurant meals we could eat. More than we could eat, as it turned out.

In those early days, Charles and I were more accustomed to cheap pensions, even flop houses, so the palatial First Class grandeur, albeit faded, of the Hotel Beke on Budapest's broad, tree-lined Lenin Korut really impressed us. We were required to have separate rooms – more hard currency for the state, obviously – and these proved to be high-ceilinged affairs, filled with traditional style furniture. Our windows, with their slightly tattered lace curtains, overlooked a small garden courtyard.

As we had this seemingly endless supply of meal vouchers which were redeemable at virtually any state-owned restaurant (which meant *any* restaurant, since all were state owned), we ate like Party Commissars. Even so, by our last night in Budapest we still had bundles of nonrefundable meal vouchers. Naturally, being two young fellows accustomed to having to pinch pennies, we determined that as we couldn't get a refund on our unused coupons, we could at least do our level best to eat and drink up as much of the remaining horde of vouchers as might prove possible. For our herculean effort, we repaired to the Hotel Beke's atmospheric basement restaurant known as the Wine Cellar. Vaulted brick walls and ceilings, candlelit tables, a gypsy orchestra playing that frantic, haunting Magyar music as though their lives depended on it (and that may well have been the case) – this was the scene awaiting us and our meal vouchers.

We ordered everything, including (but not restricted to) Russian caviar, the finest wines, goulash, chicken paprika, the delectable fogash fish from the Danube, cheese, coffee and liqueurs.

Budapest: Eating like Party commissars

We were at the end of a long table, and sitting at the other end was a slim, fiftyish man with thinning, slicked-back hair and wearing a long, black leather coat even as he ate his dinner. At first, he had even worn his Gestapo-style black fedora as he ate. He watched us like a cat observing canaries. If this guy wasn't from the AVO, the Hungarian equivalent of the KGB, I'd eat my goulash. Except that I had already done that. The creature spoke, and in English. "You . . .eat . . .well!" he declared, smirking as he hovered over a bowl of borscht. He had no way of knowing that we were Hungarian food coupon Rockefellers. He probably thought this was but a mere snack for a couple of capitalist running dogs, paid for by funds accumulated from the tattered coin purses snatched from starving grandmothers of destitute workers.

"Mmmmf," we both said, looking at the guy, but not pausing in our determined mastication.

We departed Budapest by train the next day and didn't eat anything else for twenty-four hours. But when we did start eating again, we would sometimes look, frowning, at each other during a meal and grunt in unison, our mouths full, "You . . .eat . . .well!" Then, mouths still full, we'd die laughing.

SPIES ON THE DALMATION COAST

When brother Charles and I climbed down from the train at the Dalmation Coast town of Split, we took an immediate liking to the place and decided to stick around for a few days. Split, or Spoleto when it was still part of the Roman Empire, was an interesting mix of the ancient and the almost-modern. In the very center of the city, the former palace of the Emperor Diocletian, built about 300 A.D., was still very much in use, not by Romans, but by hundreds of poor Croat families who had turned the big, crumbling stone edifice which faced the sea into a sort of Yugoslav tenement. Palm trees lined the scooter-clogged streets, and a warm October sun shone down on everything.

A toothless old crone at the railroad station had pitched her *pensione* to us in a sort of Italian, enough for me to get the gist, anyway, and the price seemed right, so we agreed to stay with her. We paid the equivalent of a dollar twenty-five U.S. per day for a pleasant room with a big double bed, plus breakfast and dinner with local wine, served at the kitchen table by the crone herself. Despite Yugoslavia's official status as an atheist communist state, our whitewashed room had three or four framed religious pictures cut from magazines hanging on the walls.

Our digs were in a cheap, modern block of apartments which we referred to as "the project," located two or three miles out from the center of Split, a short ride by municipal bus. The Adriatic Sea was not far away, and although there was no beach there, we went swimming from the big gray rocks which lined the coast. At night, tired from a day of exploring the sun-baked town, swimming in the sea, and socializing over glasses of local wine in cheap terrace cafes of the town, we would retire to our lodgings and drift off to sleep to the sound of a bunch of drunks singing endless choruses of *Ave Maria* from a nearby apartment block. The singing was sort of raucous, yet at the same time rather pleasant.

On about our third day in Split, we walked farther north along the coast than we had yet been. A recently degree-conferred commercial art student, I had my ever-present small sketchbook with me, along with my German rapidograph pen, a source of smooth-flowing India ink, with a very nice, fine line. I would occasionally stop and do a sketch of whatever caught my interest, and Charles would demonstrate admirable patience as I did so.

We walked along what appeared to be cow or goat trails through scrub-covered hills, the Adriatic on one side, and severe, gray mountains on the other. After a while, we came to a barbed wire fence and a crude gate beside which a sign in Serbo-Croat announced something totally unintelligible to us. We went on through, as the gate was open and no one was around.

Topping a hill, we gazed down into a long, narrow, steep-sided body of water I can describe only as a fjord. And in the fjord were several warships: surfaced submarines, destroyers, PT boats and more. We stared for a moment, then looked at each other. Charles spoke first.

"I got a feeling we're not supposed to be looking at this."

"Umh," I replied. "Let's get out of here."

We turned and headed back the way we had come, but before we had taken ten steps, a huge motorcycle roared up the goat track, apparently having come out from under a rock. Riding it was a uniformed and helmeted soldier, who yelled at us in Serbo-Croat.

Having no idea what the man was saying, we just shrugged and responded in English. The uniformed man then pulled a huge pistol from his holster and pointed it at us, now talking louder and more excitedly. He pointed back down the track, indicating that we should go that way. Needless to say, we did.

The cycle cop directed us to a military installation built of unpainted cement blocks in a little valley close by. Several uniformed types came out and took turns trying to ask us questions, but none spoke English, or apparently anything else other than Serbo-Croat.

Split: Spies on the Dalmatian Coast

Exasperated, they took us inside and searched us, finding our American passports. One word I did understand because it sounded like Russian: *Spioni*. They thought we were spies.

One of the soldiers found my sketchbook which contained only innocuous drawings of downtown Split, the seacoast and "the project," but it didn't take much to figure out that these guys were undoubtedly saying to themselves, yeah, and the only reason there aren't any sketches of our warships in the fjord is because we caught these spies in time.

"I wonder what do we do now," I said.

"Just act stupid," Charles replied.

"That'll be easy," I sighed.

We spent the next five days in a Yugoslav military jail cell answering questions posed by an English-speaking officer they had finally found someplace. Apparently they became satisfied after a while that we were telling the truth, as they let us go. We trudged back to "the project," but word had quite obviously preceded us, because when we got to the front door of our apartment, where the rent had been paid in advance, we found all our belongings piled outside against the wall.

We gathered up our stuff and blew town. Blew Yugoslavia, for that matter.

On another occasion I was in Zagreb, in northern Yugoslavia (now Croatia), when some big shots came to town. Josip Broz, better known as Tito, was the communist dictator of Yugoslavia, while Nikita Khrushchev was First Secretary, or Boss, of the Soviet Union, and Leonid Brezhnev was Chairman of the Presidium of the Supreme Soviet of the Soviet Union or Second Fiddle.

Yugoslavia at this time was, while a communist state, a sort of rebel entity as regards Moscow – and a gadfly to the USSR. Brezhnev was coming to visit, ostensibly to make a speech at an event hailing a rare joint Soviet-Yugoslav agricultural project in the Zagreb area, but most likely to try to effect a "thaw" with the ornery Yugoslavs. President Tito was coming from Belgrade. It would be a grand occasion.

I learned that Brezhnev was arriving by a special blue train, and Tito would meet him at the railroad station. Then the two great ones would ride in parade up the avenue which ran from the station to the city's main square and the local Party headquarters. As the appointed time approached, I walked to the parade avenue, where big crowds were gathering, and I found a place at the curb. I happened to be standing next to a youngish man who, noting my clothes and general appearance, asked if I were an American. I said yes, and he identified himself as a Dane, in town on business. We began chatting, and when a teenaged Party worker came by with a basket full of paper Soviet and Yugoslav flags, we each took one of the latter and practiced waving them.

The parade route was along a pleasant, wide, tree-lined boulevard, and from the lower end, near the rail station, we heard cheering and a band playing. Soon the official automobiles, three black Russian Zils resembling 1948 Packards, approached, and everyone began frantically waving their paper flags. The car with Brezhnev and Tito in the back seat, a convertible, glided past, the two men sitting stolidly in their seats, immobile and unsmiling. Not even a Queen Elizabeth-style faint wave.

Next came the marching band, a Yugoslav army unit, and they were playing . . .*The Stars and Stripes Forever!* Even my new friend the Dane knew that was a U.S. piece, and we both started laughing and talking about how weird that was – John Philip Sousa's immortal American march being played by a communist army band for two Party leaders. At that point, a fortyish man behind us (our heretofore secret minder?) tugged at my sleeve and said, in heavily accented English, "That is famous Russian march song!" The Dane and I looked at each other and tried to keep straight faces. How silly of us. Of course it was a Russian song. And, naturally, a Russian had written it. After all, didn't a Russian invent the electric light bulb, the telephone, the airplane, radio and TV? The real name of the marching song was probably *The Hammer* and *Sickle Forever*. And the band played on.

YOUR PAPERS ARE NOT IN ORDER!

When one took a train from a Western European country into one of the Communist Bloc countries, there was no doubt whatsoever when the border was crossed, if you were looking out the window. First came a clear-cut area, then a series of barbed wire fences and watchtowers with submachinegun-wielding border guards. Sometimes there was a tank or armored car at the checkpoint. If you crossed the border by bus, the communist border police would inspect the inside of the coach, looking for forbidden items, including such innocuous things as *Time* or *Newsweek* magazines. Other guards would be restraining ferocious-looking German shepherds, while still others probed under the bus with mirrors on long poles, making sure no one was hiding himself up under the vehicle.

Traveling by train in Eastern Europe was pretty much like that in most of Western Europe, except that the coaches seemed to be rattier and the border police and customs officials much more authoritative, even rude. More than once in East Germany I encountered a female police official, each of them old bag commies dressed like Hollywood's concept of an evil hag, wearing a long dress that looked as though it had been made at home out of worn out draperies, and with a face like the Wicked Witch of the West. These, er, ladies apparently wanted to be sure no one could accuse them of being soft on capitalist pigs – or on anybody, for that matter. Their interest was in you and your passport; no spies would slip by. The bag inspections were of course left to the uniformed customs officers. One of them found a small transistor radio in my bag, and he debated confiscating it for quite some time. Happily, he was distracted when some sort of ruckus erupted further down the car, whereupon he tossed my radio onto the seat and rushed out of my compartment.

Once the border formalities were done, you would enter a region of farms with dilapidated houses and barns, and usually with a farmer, possibly in traditional national attire, plowing his land behind a horse or mule. Tractors hadn't made it to individual farms yet. If you were traveling in autumn, you might well see peasant comrades "stomping out" grapes in a big half-barrel.

Your compartment companions were most likely to be Westerners traveling east on business, although occasionally there would be locals going home, those lucky ones allowed to leave earlier, although almost certainly there would have been family members left behind as hostages, to encourage the travelers' return. Traditionally, they would have their basket of sausage, cheese, bread and wine or vodka, and they would dine en route. Unlike the Spanish, they didn't usually offer you some of their food.

In the earliest days, when I traveled with my brother, we would sometimes board a train and find a compartment empty of other travelers. After the train got underway, if no one else had come along and entered our compartment, we would of course have it completely to ourselves. Then, when the train made further stops along the way and a few new passengers boarded, we might endeavor to keep the compartment for ourselves through a little play-acting. If someone slid open the door, looking for a seat, we were known to start yelling loudly at each other, as though we were on the brink of a fight. The seat-seeker almost always moved on to another compartment.

If you arrived in an Eastern European city in winter, you would immediately smell the soot in the air. Soft coal was used for heating and power throughout this region. As a result, the buildings were all pitch black. If you arrived in summer, probably the first thing you would smell would be the people. Bathing was obviously not a top priority in the east. It was worst when you were on a crowded tram or bus on a warm day.

Big Brother was always lurking out there. I was in a train station in Dresden, East Germany, one time, waiting on the platform for my train, when a voice which sounded like that of a female top sergeant on the parade ground suddenly boomed out of a loudspeaker: "You there! You in the blue overcoat! Put out that cigarette! This is a no smoking area! You will not be warned again!" I am sure the poor guy in the blue overcoat did as he was told, then rushed to the men's room to change his pants.

A HAVEN IN PRAGUE

Eastern Europeans seemed, understandably, wary of all strangers. After all, in East Germany you could be an agent of the Stasi, or in Hungary an AVO thug. Or, especially in Czechoslovakia, you might be a German. The Czechs did not like Germans. World War II wasn't all that long ago, and they remembered. I was in Prague one time on business, and I was walking along Wenceslas Square one evening. It was dark, snowing and very cold. I had finished my meetings and was going back to my hotel, the Alcron. Prague was closed for the night, the sidewalks rolled up and shop windows shuttered. Then I heard violin music close by; it emanated from a tiny tavern, and light from the small pane in the top half of a wooden door told me the place was open, so I went inside.

The place was, as I say, tiny, probably no more than 25 feet square. There was a very small bar in a far corner, and maybe six old battered tables, all of which were occupied by worker types, all men. Three violinists stood against one wall; it was their music I had heard – Smetana, as it turned out. When I walked in, shutting the door behind me, it was like one of those western movies when the stranger walks into the saloon and instantly all talking ceases and the pianist stops playing. Silence, with everybody staring at me. Self consciously, I walked to the bar, ordering beer in German. Still nobody spoke, nor did the musicians resume playing. The young bartender drew me a beer, then asked me in German where I was from, and I replied, "America." The bartender's eyebrows shot up and he turned and shouted out, "American!" The whole place erupted in cheers, and several of the men got up from their tables and came up to me, slapping me on the shoulder and shaking my hand. Everybody was now talking again, and the violinists resumed their playing. What an experience.

As it turned out, the musicians played for the Prague Symphony Orchestra, and they invited me to come to a performance the next night at the concert hall, giving me a free pass. (I went, and it was wonderful, an evening devoted to the works of Smetana.) Another man invited me to come to his flat and let him fix supper for me. I tried to politely decline, but he begged me profusely, saying that he had not had anyone with whom to speak English in so long. Would I not please come, and I could tell him what was really going on outside the borders of Czechoslovakia. I finally gave in, and I am glad I did, as it was a most pleasurable evening. The man cooked us each a tiny steak, of which he was obviously very proud. I returned to my hotel feeling really good.

A PEEK BEHIND THE CURTAIN

All U.S. tour groups visiting West Berlin of course wanted "a peek behind the Iron Curtain" by going into East Berlin. It became a bit more difficult after the Wall went up in 1961, but it was still possible for bona fide Western tourists. The tour bus would go through from West Berlin at Checkpoint Charlie, in the American sector of the city. A serious system of barbed wire fences and concrete baffles had been erected by the East Germans, under the watchful eyes of their Soviet masters. Then came the massive Wall itself, and once through that the bus would stop and an East German Vopo (short for *Volkspolizei* – People's Police) would come onto the bus, checking passports and keeping an eye out for those subversive publications. Western newspapers and magazines were seized and taken away.

One Vopo had apparently not had a bath in months, maybe years. The stench he left behind was overpowering. When he finally exited the now-stinking bus, one of the group quipped, "He's still with us!" Everybody roared with laughter. Unfortunately, the smelly Vopo heard the laughing and realized it had to do with him. Furious, he remounted the coach and let it be known that the *verdammt* tourists would have to pay for their insolence, punishment coming in the form of a very long delay before the driver was given permission to crank the bus up again and continue on into East Berlin.

East Berlin: The smelly Vopo with subversive literature

Once behind the still-new Wall, Vopos were everywhere, as were still-demolished structures, ruins left over from World War II. The main streets tended to sport new or cheaply rebuilt buildings, but a glance down the side streets revealed windowless walls, rubble, broken beams sticking up into the sky, and boarded up doorways and windows in walls still standing.

In East Berlin, as in so many cities of East Germany, there was a street called 8 Mai Strasse. The eighth of May, 1945, was of course the day Germany surrendered. Or in the local parlance, the day Germany was finally totally liberated by the Russians. Thus East Germany was the only country I had ever known of which celebrated the day of its own defeat.

An East German guide was put onto the bus for the tour of the communist sector, and tourists got an earful of Party propaganda. Snickers from the passengers were common, garnering fearsome glares from the faithful Party guide. The tour included the great cemetery for Soviet soldiers killed in the Battle for Berlin, and other Russian-oriented places. At least one good stop was at the great Pergamum Museum, with Schliemann's relics of Troy. But everything else in the heart of old pre-war Berlin, including the cathedral and the other old buildings of the Lustgarten, were still hollow, blackened shells. The people on the tour were usually very happy to get back to West Berlin.

After doing the East Berlin tour a few times, I decided on one occasion to "sit this one out" after we passed through Checkpoint Charlie. I was the trip escort, not the guide, so I was not needed for this part. With me was one of my co-workers, as this was a group involving two buses, and we decided to pass the tour time just hanging out in East Berlin. The best hotel in that part of town in those days was a real dump of a place, the Russian-built Hotel Berolina. A Russian-built hotel meant that if you were a guest and went into your room for the first time and tried to turn on the lights from a wall switch, there was a good chance the whole switch box would simply fall out of the wall. Just as the wall-mounted soap dish in the bathroom might fall off as soon as you touched it. And the thermostat wouldn't work, and the toilet wouldn't flush. Ah, Russian hotels.

Anyway, my colleague Sharon and I weren't looking for a room, we just went to the depressing little bar, to get beers and have a chat. I got two drafts at the counter and took them to a small table. At the bar were two men, maybe East Germans, maybe Russians. They and the bartender seemed most interested in the conversation in English which Sharon and I were having, and making no bones about it, staring intently at us. After a few minutes, the bartender went into a back room and returned with one of those old hand-cranked phonograph machines like my grandfather used to have. Smiling a big smile, he produced an old 78 rpm record and put it on the turntable. Then he cranked up the old Victrola or whatever it was and lowered the needle onto the record. There were a few scratchy sounds, then the tinny voices of men singing in English, but with a heavy German accent:

She'll be koaming 'round ze mountain ven she koams,
She'll be koaming 'round ze mountain ven she koams . . .

Sharon and I both looked amazed, and then we both died laughing. The bartender seemed to take this as a good sign, as he smiled even broader. Even the two dour patrons at the bar cracked half-smiles.

But all was not laughs in Berlin. When I was there just after the Wall went up, attempted escapes from East Berlin were big in the news. I went to a place on the western side of the Wall where there was a huge pile of flowers at the spot where, on the Wall's other side a few days earlier, a German youth named Peter Fechter had tried to make his escape over the barrier but had been shot down by Vopos in guard towers. The young man had lain on the ground on the eastern side, mortally wounded but crying out for help for hours, while the Vopos did nothing, just letting him finally die. The West Berlin police had to forcefully restrain crowds of angry young West Berliners, who wanted to storm the Wall, to try to save the youth. Something like that simply could not be allowed, lest it spark an East-West confrontation possibly resulting in World War III.

6

The Soviet Union: The Operative Word Was "Nyet!"

HOTELS AND RESTAURANTS IN THE USSR

People on group tours to the Soviet Union almost always ate all meals in their hotel's dining room. There was no selection. You would take every meal in the same gigantic dining hall, along with hundreds – maybe thousands – of members of other tour groups from all over the Western world. (No Bulgarian or Polish groups – they stayed and ate at very inferior hotels for comrades-only.) Your breakfast might consist of a sort of plain hot dog with nothing on it, a blini (small pancake), black bread and a glass of pink and unsalted tomato juice (horrible), plus coffee or tea. Lunch and dinner were usually virtually identical: a bowl of bortsch, some sort of beef stroganoff with steamed red cabbage, and water. You could order a beer for which you would have to pay in Western currency upon delivery, if it ever came. Dessert might be a scoop of ice cream or a tough pastry.

Now, if you were traveling on your own and wanted desperately to eat anywhere other than in that depressing, cattle-pen hotel dining room – and assuming you had your meal vouchers – you could theoretically dine at any of the state-run restaurants scattered about the city. That is, if you could find one open. And even if you located one which was apparently open for business, because you could see people inside, eating, you very well might find the front door locked. This was because the employees inside just didn't want to have to bother with more customers. They got paid the same, whether they served many people or none at all. They were forbidden to accept tips, so there was no incentive involved.

So what did you, as an individual traveler, do? You beat on the door with your fist until somebody came and looked at you through the glass and shook his finger at you,

USSR: Trying to get into a restaurant

saying, "*Nyet!*" At that point, you waved your American (or British, or French, or whatever Western country) passport at him and frowned. The door would then be opened and you would reluctantly be shown to a table.

Then you would be given a menu written in Russian. If you were lucky, this restaurant's menu might have a small English translation under the Cyrillic. And the listings might be impressive, with long columns showing smoked sturgeon, chicken Kiev, shashlik, beluga caviar, and on and on. But the trick was to look for a dish listed with the price written in, out to the side, because those were the only dishes actually available. Two hundred dishes might be listed on the menu, but only two might really be obtainable. And they would most likely be some variety of greasy roasted chicken – all skin and bones, no meat – plus a watery chicken soup that the chicken apparently just walked through without stopping. These restaurants did usually had excellent bread rolls and if they had ice cream (vanilla or chocolate only), it was very good, too.

I had to arrange cocktail parties for many of my groups to the USSR, and would explain to them up front not to expect an American style bash. The Russians had three categories of drinks: vodka, of course, either straight or with ice, or with canned orange juice; *champanskaya*, the "Soviet champagne," a sweet version of the very cheapest, vat-produced American bubbly; and beer, of which there was one brand: Pivo, which means "beer" in Russian.

The company for which I worked in the early days wanted me to be the person to meet with the officials of Intourist, the sole Soviet travel organization, at their offices just off Red Square in Moscow. My superiors didn't want to have to deal with the Russians face to face, while I didn't mind at all. In fact, I thought it was interesting. The

Intourist people all spoke English; they had to, to deal with the outside world.

And those people from the outside world, all Westerners, had to deal with the reality of Soviet hotels, which in those days were all built by USSR construction crews. And like everything Soviet-built, they began falling apart as soon as they opened their doors for the first time.

When, after checking in, you entered your room and reached for the light switch on the wall, there was, as mentioned earlier, a good chance the whole switchbox would simply fall out of the wall, to be left dangling by the attached wires. When you went into the bathroom to wash your hands and you reached for the pink blob of soap in the wall-mounted soap dish, the dish, like the light switch, was likely to fall off the wall and crash onto the sink, along with a wall tile or two. When you retrieved the soap and washed your hands, you quickly found that the terrible, industrial-detergent smell had permeated your skin and your hands would reek for hours. That same pink soap, never wrapped in any kind of paper, was standard at all hotels in the USSR.

There were no working controls for heating. In cold months, the heat in all hotel rooms, as well as in public areas, was stifling. In summer there was no air conditioning. Windows would not open, except for one small window in a corner, approximately one foot square – okay for winter, but murder in summer.

After using the hotel's elevators a few times, one might notice that while the spacious lobby boasted as many as six or eight elevator doors, it always seemed to be only a couple of lifts which were actually operating; the other elevator doors stayed closed, with no up-down arrows ever lit up. This was because all those other elevator doors were merely "fronts", like a Hollywood western town set. There were no shafts behind them – just a brick wall. Thus in a hotel accommodating, say, a thousand guests, the two functioning elevators would often be very overworked, and impatient crowds formed in the lobby, waiting to find a lift with room in it for them.

A few years later, the Soviet government finally admitted their workers simply could not build hotels which were up to Western standards, and they began hiring construction firms from West Germany, France, Finland, Japan and other non-communist countries. And these new hotels were what Westerners expected.

I experienced a wild scene in the big group dining hall of the Hotel Intourist in Moscow. I was having dinner with my group when I heard much shouting in German coming from a group located a few tables away. A man was standing and shouting, pointing at a man at another table at which sat a different West German group. A crowd of dining room personnel formed around the area, along with a couple of hotel security men. More shouting, then uniformed militia (local police) showed up and, finally, the man at the second table was taken away. I later learned that the shouting man was a West German who had been in a Nazi concentration camp, and he had recognized the other man as a former guard at that camp. Seems the ex-guard just wanted to check out some of the places where he had served, before the Germans got pushed out of the USSR by the Red Army during that not-too-distant World War II. I never found out what happened to the former camp guard, but I doubt that it was pleasant.

THOSE BOOZY BUSINESS MEETINGS

The setup for any business meeting, anywhere in the USSR, was always the same. We would meet in a fairly large room with a big photograph of the current Party Leader – Khrushchev, then Brezhnev – on the wall. There would be two tables, one longer than the other, pushed together to form a T. The big shots sat at the head of the T, behind the shorter table, while I and several Russian flunkies sat on either side of the long table, the "trunk" of the T.

Lined up, along the center of both tables, were bottles of vodka, plus a lot of those little shot glasses. I quickly learned to get my business done in the first thirty minutes of the meeting, because half an hour in was when the Intourist official at the head of the table would suddenly cry out that it was time for the toasts. It could be 9:30 a.m., it didn't matter. Vodka would be poured all around, the flunkies doing the pouring – maybe that was their only job – then the head man would stand up and propose a toast: "To world peace!" or, "To friendship among nations!" Or such as that. And all of us would stand and knock back our drink. One after another, until everybody was laughing and the business at hand forgotten. Whew! What a way to do business! In later years, Gorbachev stopped all that, but it all held sway for a long time.

Those business meetings were sometimes nominally headed up by the big Intourist boss himself, a hulking, burly old fellow called Lebedev. I figured him to be – like so many heads of non-vital government ministries and departments – an "old fighter" loyal Party street thug with a history dating back to the days before, during and just after the Revolution of 1917-18, who had been rewarded for his faithful service with a lucrative plum in the form of the figurehead leadership of some small piece of the massive

USSR: Those boozy business meetings

Soviet government. Unlike his underlings at the meetings, Comrade Lebedev spoke no English, but he was in his element when it was time to open the vodka bottles for the many toasts. When it came to actual business matters, those English-speaking underlings – the people who really ran Intourist – were of course the ones with whom I dealt.

SEEING THE SIGHTS, SOVIET STYLE

As in all communist countries, all travel arrangements were handled by the single government travel entity – in the case of the USSR, this meant Intourist. Tour itineraries were arranged to allow virtually no free time for individuals to wander around on their own and perhaps see or do something that was not on the officially approved list.

The hotels assigned to tourists from the West (which, ironically, included Japan) were little foreign Worlds unto themselves: no Soviet or other communist country guests, only Westerners. Locals were not permitted to so much as enter the lobby of a hotel designated for foreigners; a uniformed doorman saw to that. He could pretty well spot a local by his or her clothing, but if in doubt, he would ask for the little hotel ID card provided to all guests. Locals dreamed of being able to enter such hotels, as they lusted to go into the foreign-currency shop in the lobby, which featured all sorts of imported goodies like American cigarettes, Scotch whisky, French perfume, British tape cassettes, and so on. These shops, called Beriozka shops, so named for the Russian birch tree which grows everywhere in that land, accepted only hard currencies such as American dollars, German marks, French francs, etc. The Soviet ruble was not traded on international markets, as it was in reality worthless outside the Soviet Bloc.

English was the standard foreign language in the hotels for Westerners. And at eight o'clock each Morning, every hotel lobby was packed with groups waiting to board their motorcoaches for the day's sightseeing. By nine o'clock the lobbies were all completely deserted. Nobody just dallied around the hotel during the day.

The tours were always led by a guide who was proficient in English, as well as being an indoctrinated Party-line pusher. Famous Tsarist era sites were of course pointed out, and sometimes even visited, but the guide's emphasis was always placed on how the locale related to the modern Soviet state. For example, beautiful, golden-domed St. Isaac's Cathedral in Leningrad had been turned into a museum of atheism. A lovely old former baronial palace was now the Ministry of Schlock, or whatever. Interestingly, the huge building on Moscow's Dzerzhinsky Square which housed the feared KGB was never mentioned. Although this was a busy square in the heart of the city, with the popular Detsky Mir (Children's World) store on one side, and with people coming and going, no one walked on the side of the square with the looming KGB building. Maybe they thought somebody just inside the door had a long shepherd's staff with a hook on the end, and they just might be yanked into the fearsome place's bowels.

One time, just to see what kind of response I might get, I asked our guide as we were driving past said building what it was.

"Oh, that used to be an insurance company's headquarters," she replied.

"But now it's the KGB's headquarters," I said.

"Yes, KGB." And that was all she said.

"Where they do all the washing?" I asked.

"Washing? What washing?"

"The washing of the brains," I answered, smiling. The term "brainwashing" was often in the U.S. news at the time.

The guide smiled slyly and looked at me out of the corner of an eye. "And where you may be soon," she said, still smiling. I shut up.

A GRANDE DAME OF MOSCOW

I suppose Intourist, the monolithic state travel organization of the USSR, wanted to impress me during one business trip on my part to Moscow, because the hotel accommodations they provided me with were indeed most impressive, at least by local standards of the early 1960s. I was given a large suite in the National, that old, seedily atmospheric *grande dame* hotel facing Marx Prospekt, with the red brick walls of the Kremlin looming up on the far side of the broad boulevard.

The National was not a large hotel, having only two hundred rooms, a far cry from that huge new monstrosity on the far side of Red Square called the Rossiya, with three thousand rooms, at the time the largest hotel in the world, which boasted the worst service in Moscow, the Soviet Union, and perhaps the entire planet. The National, however, still clung to a remnant of its storied past, which went back to the days of Tsar Nicholas II. During World War II it served as the American Embassy. True, everything was dingy and somewhat shabby now, and the service was certainly not what it had been before the Revolution, but it was far above that of the Rossiya and the other modern, yet already falling apart, hotels of Moscow. I loved staying at the National, reveling in its faded grandeur and appreciating its convenient central position in the city.

Many aspects of the hotel had changed since its capitalist owners had been replaced by state functionaries long ago. The high-ceilinged dining rooms on the floor above the lobby no longer bore romantic names such as the Nicholas and Alexandra Room, or the Catherine the Great Room. Now they were heroically called Halls I, II and III, and a waiter was likely to serve you the orange juice you had ordered by placing the labeled can of juice on the table in front of you, leaving it up to you to pour some into a glass. At least he would punch a couple of holes in the top of the thing before departing.

And in those days, there was always a familiar figure to be found on each floor of this hotel and in all hotels of the Soviet Union: a no-nonsense, potato-shaped lady, usually with her hair in a severe bun, who sat at a desk with a clear view down the hallways. Her official function was that of Keeper of the Keys to all the rooms on her floor, but her true identity was that of Party Snitch. She noted when you came in, when you went out, whether you were carrying anything suspicious looking, or if anyone tried to visit your room – and made notes accordingly. I never knew anyone who succeeded in taking someone of the opposite sex to his or her room, even when the whole idea was completely aboveboard, such as a man and a woman, two employees of the same firm, trying to talk business in private. And if your behavior was the teeniest bit suspect, the woman got on the horn to Comrade Dossiervitch in the Lubyanka KGB offices.

When addressing one of these women, most of whom spoke some English, since the guests were all foreigners and English was the *lingua franca*, one was well advised to refer to her proper title. Try calling her the "key lady," and you risked a lengthy and brutal tonguelashing and a reminder that she was the Floor Superintendent.

The hotel's small bar was a bit of a disappointment. It had been "modernized," and now featured a décor which was sort of a combination of 1930s art deco and Scandinavian modern, with blond wood tables and chairs with a rounded, *Metropolis*

Soviet Union hotels: The Key Lady

look. Not very pleasant, I'm afraid, and completely out of character with the rest of the hotel. Still, it was a popular gathering point for international visitors, who paid the inflated, totally artificial prices for drinks in hard currencies of the West only. As the National did not take groups, its clientele was mostly made up of foreign business and government people, in Moscow for a few days.

I never subscribed to the theory held by so many Americans visiting the USSR that virtually all the places they frequented, especially their own hotel rooms, were bugged by the KGB, but I did read many years later that the Soviet spymasters of Dzherzhinsky Square had bugged every table in the National Hotel's bar, enabling them to overhear the patrons' conversations, even ones held in very low tones. I tried desperately to remember just which political jokes I'd told to acquaintances while sitting in that bar.

The suite in the National which Intourist had given me overlooked broad Marx Prospekt and the Kremlin, and it included a large sitting room, its faded décor pre-Revolution, early twentieth century. There was a rickety loveseat, an antique writing desk with a creaky chair, tables and more creaky chairs, framed lithographs of hunting scenes from the bad old days, with dandied fops on horses, and gussied-up ladies with dainty parasols just tittering away and having a grand time. There was even a grand piano, which impressed me by its presence only, since I, not being a pianist, was hardly likely to sit down at the keyboard and in my spare moments compose some ditty which would put Tchaikovsky to shame. In any case, I couldn't have done so. Even I know that if middle C sounds like a hammer striking a lead pipe, something's wrong.

But the most astonishing item was situated near the very center of the dark, turn-of-the-century sitting room: a huge, white, full-sized refrigerator. Up to this time, hotels in the

Soviet Union had not caught up with the international trend of putting tiny refrigerator minibars in guests' rooms. This, I suppose, was the National's way of trying to see that at least the hotel's suites were up to speed, if not the rest of the rooms.

When I opened the big door to my suite's giant white fridge, at least six feet high, and found it completely empty, I was not too taken aback. What did surprise me, however, was that it was not cold at all. There was not even any water in the ice trays, much less ice. And no wonder – the machine was not plugged in. I took the electric cord and found a wall outlet, plugging the brass prongs into the little holes in the wall fixture. Immediately the refrigerator began making sounds. Loud sounds. Like a cement mixer loaded up with a full set of dishes and silverware. It was deafening. I pulled the plug.

Before retiring for the night on my last evening in Moscow, I checked at the Intourist desk in the hotel lobby to be sure my transportation to the airport was lined up for the following afternoon. Although my flight was at 7:00 p.m., the voluminous bureaucratic red tape and totalitarian harassment which were an everyday part of flying in the Soviet Union dictated that one had to plan on leaving the hotel three hours prior to flight time, much earlier than was normally required in Western cities in those pre-security days.

The bed in my suite was in a deep, curtained-off alcove around the corner from the sitting room, and there I slept. Sometime in the middle of that, my last night in Moscow, I gradually became aware of someone far off making an awful racket, banging on a door or a wall and yelling. In my sleep-numbed stupor, I decided that some drunk must be trying to get into a locked room, and I pulled the pillow over my head to try to shut out the noise. Either the drunk got into his room or went away, because the noise stopped. For a while.

Moscow: A grande dame

At some point, the hammering started again, louder now, really waking me up this time. I heard a door handle being vigorously rattled and what sounded like someone shouldering open a closed door, and then the unmistakable sound of the door to my own suite crashing open and someone stumbling in.

I sat up in bed, but before I could do anything else, the curtain to my bed alcove was whipped open, revealing a huge, shadowy human form.

"You must fly!" screamed the form in English, from the darkness. "You must fly!" Then a torrent of machinegun Russian, followed once again by, "You must fly!"

At the first "You must fly!," my only thought was, if only I could! But with the repetitions, I began to realize that this was a woman, a big woman, yes, but not a berserk KGB thug. This *grande dame* of the *grande dame* meant me no harm. On the contrary, in some bizarre way she was trying to tell me something to help me. I turned on a lamp and saw a distraught "potato lady," one of the hotel staff.

"Please," I said. "What do you mean? Slowly, please."

"You must fly! *Aeroport! Samolet!* Four o'clock! You must fly!"

Now I understood. Yes, it was four o'clock – in the morning. And yes, I did have to leave for the airport at four o'clock – but not until four o'clock that afternoon.

I explained to the potato lady and she went away. And I went back to sleep once again, at peace amidst my moldy grandeur.

THE SPY AMONGST US

The vast majority of groups my company ran to the Soviet Union were comprised of highly educated, well-traveled, upper-income people who had been everywhere else and were now giddily anticipating a probe into the spooky lair of the enemy.

I don't care how levelheaded or phlegmatic one might be back home, once he or she was plopped down on Soviet soil, spymania seized control of all brain functions, at least for most U.S. visitors I hosted. That man behind you on a Moscow sidewalk – just look at him. Carefully! Don't be obvious! You can tell he's a KGB agent! Is he the one who searched your room? Somebody did, you're positive about that. And bugged it, too – maybe through the telephone, maybe in the overhead light fixture, but not behind the cheap print on the wall. You've already checked out that possibility.

Yes, spies went everywhere with American tourists in the USSR – in their minds.

But once I was confronted with the problem of a member of one of my own groups who was believed to be a spy.

I had a full plane charter on a Pan Am 707, 178 seats and every one of them sold. We would fly into Leningrad and out of Moscow, with travel by train between the two cities, including one night in Kalinin. Kalinin (now renamed Tver) was a real dump, but the regulations governing this type of charter required stays in at least three different cities, for reasons known only to some brainless Washington bureau or agency. And Kalinin was the only place with hotel facilities between the other two cities.

The group was made up of the usual veteran travelers to other parts of the world, and thus it came as a surprise to me when I began to overhear talk that one of our members, a single lady in her fifties who had her own room and did not socialize with the others much, was, in reality, a KGB spy.

At first I took this talk as a joke, but soon I realized that most of the group members were serious. I couldn't believe it, but finally I accepted the fact that just about everybody else did. Even the elderly and mock-scholarly type, little Mr. Herman Cleghorn, the black sheep of a Fine Old Southern Family steeped in Southern Gothic politics, seemed to believe in his rare, less-enebriated moments, that the lady was a spy.

Most frustrating of all was that Phil, my company coworker on the program, who was a greatly experienced travel man ten years my elder, swallowed the spy-lady story along with everybody else.

USSR: The spy amongst us

"Phil," I pleaded, "how can you possibly think that poor lady everybody's shunning is really a KGB spy?" We were in a corner of a hotel lobby in Moscow, some five days into the trip.

"I don't know, pal," he replied, shrugging. "But you know, she does act pretty suspicious." Phil being Phil, he kept looking around for a familiar face to wave to.

"Like how?" I said.

"Well, she doesn't mix and mingle. You know, just sort of keeps to herself."

"For god's sake," I said. "Does that make her a KGB spy?"

"Well, there's other things, too," he said, squirming and looking about him. Alas, no familiar faces.

"Like what?"

"Well, just watch how she acts. She's hiding something."

I couldn't believe this. "She's not stupid, you know. She realizes everybody's calling her a spy, and she's just retreated into her shell, that's all. I feel sorry for the woman."

"Maybe so, pal, maybe so," Phil said, unconvinced. He patted my shoulder and moved away.

I made a point to try to draw the woman out a bit, arranging to sit next to her at a couple of meals and on a sightseeing tour or two. She was quiet, no doubt about that, but she was nice. She told me that she was recently widowed and had moved to a new city and knew almost no one there. When she heard about this trip to the Soviet Union, a place she'd never visited, she decided to go, thinking that perhaps it would do her good. But it had been a mistake, she said. Now she was just the butt of a stupid and cruel joke, and nobody would have anything to do with her. They just whispered silly things behind her back and cast suspicious glances at her. She wanted to go home.

I did what I could to undo this tragic stupidity, promulgated and perpetrated by a group of otherwise intelligent people, candidly retelling the lady's tale to one and all, and within a couple of days most had relegated the whole business to joke status. Even Phil finally accepted it as just a funny episode, but he, like the others, now missed the drama of having a KGB spy in our midst.

However, there were still a few diehards in the group who vigorously opposed the idea of abandoning the lady spy watch. So it was for them more than anyone – though also for the whole group, really – that I persuaded Phil we should, as a group, *elect* the true spy, thus officially turning the thing into buffoonery.

At the final evening dinner in a private dining salon on the top floor of Moscow's Intourist Hotel, Phil rapped for attention on his water glass with a knife and then announced that during the course of the evening everyone was requested to write down on a piece of paper the name of the person whom they felt was the true KGB spy in our midst. Everyone responded eagerly, and a hat was subsequently passed to collect all the paper ballots. In the meantime, iced vodka, followed by lots of the sweet, bulk-processed Soviet *champanskaya* flowed, loosening tongues and making the main course, the school cafeteria grade beef stroganoff, at least edible. And in the interim, Phil and I tabulated the ballots, with a surprising result.

Phil rose to announce the revelation of the spy, dinging on a glass for attention. The room grew hushed. Though he did not mention it, the lady who had been the butt of all the earlier foolishness garnered only three votes in the end. The overwhelming winner, with sixty-six of the possible one hundred and seventy eight votes, was none other than Mr.

Herman Cleghorn, the booze-soaked scion of the Fine Old Southern Family known for its eloquent politicians.

A great cheer went up, and cries of "Speech! Speech!" urged the emaciated and diminutive Mr. Cleghorn to officially accept his newly bestowed title. Alas, Mr. Cleghorn was far too well imbued with vodka and Soviet *champanskaya* to respond properly, though he was apparently conscious, simply sitting in his seat and grinning moronically without a clue as to what was happening. He did seem to be aware that everyone was looking at him and smiling, so he smiled back, even attempting a little House of Windsor wave to his adoring masses. Then he slowly fell forward until he had deposited his face into his dessert *blinz*.

The crowd cheered. At last we had our spy.

I WAS AN FBI INFORMANT . . . AND MORE

On the other side of the Atlantic, I have to admit I was aware that some spy business really did happen. Whenever representatives of the Soviet travel organization Intourist came to Atlanta to call on me and make a sales pitch for a "new" destination within the USSR, their visit would always be followed by a "social call" to my office on the part of two dour FBI agents who wanted to know exactly what was said, hinted at, or imagined by the visiting Russians – and by me. All Intourist officials, they told me, were master spies. It was my duty as a loyal American to tell all. So, of course, I did so willingly, although I never had anything of interest to report.

Sometimes, though, the spying was funny. One time at the Atlanta airport, I met a couple of Russians coming off a flight from Miami, where they had been on business. They were the only two men on the flight wearing coats and ties.

Everybody else wore tropical resort wear on this warm day in early spring, with one other exception. The last guy off the plane, who was in his late thirties and wearing a wool pullover sweater which I imagine he put on that morning in chilly Washington, D.C., prior to flying to Miami to commence a "tailing" job, nonchalantly sauntered along behind the two Russians at a distance of perhaps twenty yards. I saw him later in the baggage claim area, although he apparently had no luggage of his own, and I saw him again in the lobby of the downtown hotel while the Russians were checking in. About as subtle as a club, I said to myself, and I could only reason that he wanted the Intourist men to know he was shadowing them. Although the Russians never said anything to me about this, they did make joking references to it in Russian between themselves.

On another occasion, while at dinner at a suburban Atlanta restaurant with the head of Intourist's New York office, I asked my Russian friend why he was chuckling. He replied that his FBI "tail," whom he identified as a thirty-something man dining solo against the far wall, was just so obvious as to be laughable. Perhaps unwisely, I stared at the man – but he studiously refrained from looking my way.

Episodes like this apparently turned me into a subversive. At least, that's the way those humor-starved agents of the FBI would probably look at it. You see, even today, if you close the door to my office, you will observe on the wall behind the door a framed portrait of George Washington. A small clasp at the bottom permits the hinged picture to

USA: I was an informant for the FBI . . . and more

be swung out, revealing behind it another one, this one a portrait of Vladimir Ilyich Lenin, posturing before a yellow hammer-and-sickle on a red field.

The FBI boys would not be amused.

Spy mania even reached into (and onto) my own home. Upon returning from one of my early trips to the Soviet Union, as I approached the front door of my home, suitcase in hand, I noticed on a window pane a strange object, trailing a wire. I took a look and found one of those small, cheap microphones of the type used with inexpensive cassette recorders, stuck to the window with duct tape. An electric wire ran from the device down and into the ground. I untaped the microphone from the window pane and checked it out. A sticker label was affixed to the mike; in Cyrillic Russian alphabet letters, a handwritten notice read, *Made in Moscow – Speak Loud*. My jokester brother at work.

7

Was Getting There
Really Half the Fun?

TRAINS, PLANES AND
AUTOMOBILES – AND BOATS

Go back far enough, and it seemed that just about everybody who went to Europe traveled "by boat", or, more correctly, by steamship. That's the way I went my first time, and I remember observing from the deck of the Cunard Line's *Mauretania* all those other big ships – there must have been twenty of them – docked along the west side of Manhattan Island, preparing to sail to such ports as Cobh (for Ireland), Southampton, Le Havre, Bremerhaven, Lisbon, Gibraltar, Barcelona, Genoa, Naples and Piraeus. The steamship lines' motto was "Getting there is half the fun!" and it could indeed be fun on a big ship, sailing transatlantic for a week or so, with plenty of time for meeting other young Americans. Movies, dancing, shipboard romances – like I say, fun. Transatlantic steamships' passenger decks were broken down into three classes: First, Cabin, and Tourist. It seemed that when you descended from First Class, up top, the designation of accommodations changed from "staterooms" to "cabins". "Cubbyholes" would have been a more appropriate label for many of those cubicles in Tourist Class. The lower down you went in any ship, the more inside cabins (no porthole) you found. And as ships were not air conditioned in those early days, an inside cabin could become quite stuffy, especially in summertime. When I thought about those non-air-conditioned ships taking

A Dirt Cheap (and Different) World

passengers on cruises to tropical areas of the world when it
was wintertime in the northern hemisphere, I immediately
broke out in a sweat.

There were of course bars and restaurants in all three
classes of all ships, and entertainment, as well. But it will
come as no surprise to learn that the higher up one went,
the bars, dining rooms and after-dinner entertainment got
progressively better. Ditto for deck facilities: swimming
pools, deck games, etc. So, naturally, it became a challenge
for the younger Tourist Class passengers to somehow slip up
to First Class without being spotted by the tux-or-dinner-
jacketed steward posted like a guard at the top of each
stairway leading to a higher class. Getting by these fellows
was tricky, but it could be done; best to be wearing one's best
duds, however. At least there was no punishment for being
caught, other than a hasty return to the bowels of the ship.

Not as much fun but slightly quicker was the method
I used the second time I went to Europe: by air. I had
gotten a job in Spain through a student exchange program,
and part of the deal was a cheap flight to Europe from
Newark. I took the train from Atlanta to Newark and there,
after a lengthy delay, I boarded a chartered DC-4 of Seven
Seas Airlines. The DC-4 was an unpressurized aircraft,
not exactly ideal for flying transatlantic, but pressurization
wouldn't have worked with our plane, anyway, because the
door wouldn't close all the way. The hinges were sprung, or
something, and the door had to be lashed as shut as it would
go, using a thick, hawser-like rope, leaving a gap of about
four inches. As a result, there was a virtual wind tunnel
through the fuselage, maybe because the pilot had cracked
his side window, to let out his cigarette smoke. I suppose this
had something to do with the fact that we flew very low all
the way across the Atlantic, like 2000 feet or so. Peering out

the big crack at the lashed-almost-shut door while in flight, you could see people walking around on ships, below.

A DC-4 is supposed to have two-and-two seating, but this plane had an extra seat for each row, meaning a two-and-three configuration. I was in an aisle seat and at one point it simply fell out into the aisle. The flimsy seats were made to be easily removable, to convert the aircraft to an all-cargo mode; mine moved *too* easily. An extra seat per row of course meant a very narrow aisle; indeed, one had to proceed down it sideways, and no meal cart could possibly navigate it.

The pilot was a German . . . who appeared none too trustworthy; he needed a shave and wore a pistol on his hip. The navigator was from Ghana, a tall, thin man who always had a pint of liquor poking out of a back pants pocket. And the one stewardess, an Australian lass whom one might say had "been around the block," had so much stainless steel metal work in her mouth that I swear her face always pointed north. She served us one meal, and when she brought me my tray, everything was frozen solid.

Our flight plan took us to seemingly every bit of land or solid rock or ice between Newark and Amsterdam, our final destination. We stopped in Bangor, Gander, Reykjavik and Shannon, before finally arriving in Amsterdam. Trip time was twenty-one hours.

Years later, upon reading a book entitled *The Arms Merchants*, I learned that Seven Seas Airlines was a notorious gun-running operation based in Luxembourg. While we had been waiting for our delayed flight in Newark, we had been told that the plane was late because it had been flying nuns from the civil war-plagued ex-Belgian Congo to Brussels. Maybe so, but, clearly, the reason for flying to the Belgian Congo in the first place had been to run in a planeload of guns for Moise Tshombe's white mercenary-led rebels in the mineral-rich Katanga province, who were fighting for independence from the newly-formed Republic of the Congo.

By the way, when we made our stop in Gander, Newfoundland, the terminal was a huge, cold and drafty old quonset hut with a few wooden chairs and a small, crudely-built snack bar in the center which sold whale blubber sandwiches or something like that. A year later, a brand new, modern style terminal opened in Gander, to service the many flights between America and Europe which made necessary refueling stops there. Ironically, the very year the new terminal was inaugurated, jet passenger planes went into service – and these new aircraft did not require a refueling stop in Gander. Some Newfi politician blew it.

In places where weather was not a big factor in outdoor activities, airports would sometimes have open-air terrace cafes near or actually on the tarmac, for people waiting to board a flight or to meet arriving passengers. They were usually separated from the area of the aircraft themselves by little fences maybe three feet high. Finish your snack or drink, pay your tab, and then pass through the little gate and walk over to your plane and mount the rolling staircase. No security check, of course.

The planeside terrace café at Piarco Airport in Port-of-Spain, Trinidad, also offered a live band in the evening, and dancing under the stars. It was there that I saw my first passenger jet, a Comet of BOAC from London.

At the in-city airport of Congonhas in São Paulo, Brazil, the terrace cafe was so close to the parked Constellations that a wingtip would sometimes be protruding into the café's airspace. This place was elaborately decorated with big potted palms and tropical flower plants. It made waiting for your plane very pleasant – unless a departing aircraft turned just so, and you got a stiff wind in the face from the prop wash.

FLYING THE FUNKY SKIES OF AEROFLOT

Especially in Europe, I didn't do too much flying in those days, although some areas, such as the vast USSR, left little alternative. The Soviet Union boasted a single, government owned and operated airline, Aeroflot, world renowned for its huge fleet of buckets of bolts which never required maintenance. Travel by domestic flight service of Aeroflot throughout the Workers' Paradise involved one class of service only – thus no elitism, theoretically. You see, if you were a foreigner from outside the Communist Bloc, and a Westerner in particular, you got something declared to be First Class treatment at coach class prices. Cheap coach class prices. And First Class treatment by old Soviet standards.

Actually, it would be more accurate to say that you got special treatment before and after the flight, because, in truth, everybody got the same kind of seat on the plane – as well as the same meal service, which was none. When a foreigner from a capitalist country checked in for a domestic flight, he or she was shown to a special, foreigners-only waiting room which was inevitably smaller but much nicer than the facilities afforded to the citizens of the USSR. Generally it was supervised by a uniformed female staffer who might, in extreme circumstances, permit a ghost of a smile to pass across her face, whereas any personnel working the comrades' barn-like holding tank on the other side of the wall were apparently forbidden by Soviet law to smile or exhibit any human traits whatsoever – unless wielding a bludgeon for crowd control counted. There might even be padded chairs or sofas for the foreigners to sit on. Sometimes this waiting area offered tea, dispensed from a big stainless steel samovar made in Tula, to make perusal of *The Collected Speeches of V. I. Lenin* or other such available literature on the reading rack that much more enjoyable. Magazines or newspapers brought in from the West had, of course, been confiscated upon the foreigner's arrival in the USSR. (Hemingway and Jack London were two of the very few popular U.S. authors whose writings were admitted.)

Naturally, the Soviet authorities wanted to impress foreigners, but there was more to the segregation situation than that. The main idea was to create a protective, prophylactic insulation between their citizens and outsiders with dangerous ideas to disseminate. Like wash-n-wear clothes, small transistor radios and fancy cameras. And, of course, there was the ever-present danger that actual conversation might take place between representatives of the two different worlds. There might be talk about America and private homes, two-car families, three-car families, even four-car families. But no one would believe that.

On one trip, I was shown into one of these isolation chambers at the air terminal in Simferopol in the Crimea – the airport for Yalta, Alupka and other sundrenched coastal resorts along the Black Sea, some sixty miles to the south of the city. This particular foreigners-only waiting room was nicer than most and staffed by two young ladies in their mid-twenties who were also friendlier than the average Soviet personnel, and certainly more outgoing. And very curious. And with some really crazy ideas about America and Americans.

I was the only alien present at the time, so I had the lounge to myself as I waited for my flight to be called. Although I was trying to get some paperwork done, the two girls flitted around me as though I were a Hollywood movie star, making concentration impossible. As I found out, they spoke surprisingly good English.

"Are you married?" one asked me, leaning close. I said I was.

"Do you love your wife?" asked the other one. Flustered, I again replied in the affirmative, adding, "of course."

"How long have you been married?" I mentally counted back and finally replied three and a half years. The girls gasped and looked at each other, then back at me.

"But we were told all Americans get divorced after a year," the first girl said. They both looked at me warily, apparently having decided I spoke with forked tongue. I assured them this was not the case.

"Is it true Americans eat only synthetic food?" the second girl said.

"What?" I said.

"We were told Americans do not eat meat or vegetables or fruit as we do. Only food made from chemicals in laboratories. Is this true?"

"Look, I don't know where –" At that moment my flight was called. I hastily gathered up my belongings and made for the exit, bidding the two curious girls *dosvidanya* and blowing out a sigh of mystification. I doubted my powers to persuade them that America was indeed not a land of two hundred million divorced people subsisting on synthetic food from some mad scientist's laboratory.

In Simferopol, as everywhere else in the USSR, my journey from air terminal to aircraft involved a set procedure: I exited the lounge through a special door and boarded an ancient waiting bus that was also for foreigners only, and it took me out to the plane. Sometimes I was the only person on the whole bus. In the meantime, the rest of the plane's passengers – mostly Soviet citizens, with maybe a Bulgarian or two thrown in – would be packed into another old bus for their separate and unequal ride out to the plane.

Foreigners were supposed to board first. Usually the aliens' bus arrived at the aircraft before the other bus did, and then you just clambered aboard and picked out a seat, any seat, to your liking. There were no seat assignments, and all seats were pretty much the same. None got any meal service. And all seats were no smoking, long before the movement caught on elsewhere. But it wasn't because the Soviets were ahead of the times healthwise. If they had allowed smoking aboard the plane, the fuselage would have been so thick with smoke ten minutes after takeoff that if someone had cracked a window, the aircraft would have left a smoke contrail behind it like a skywriter plane. And ten minutes after that, everyone aboard would have been dead and fully smoke-cured.

If the foreigners' bus did not arrive at the aircraft before the locals' bus, the Russians were required to wait at the foot of the mobile staircase until the foreigners showed. Inevitably in such cases, they would crowd the bottom of the steps, maybe two hundred of them pushing each other as they tried to inch closer. When the non-Soviets or, in the case of my flight out of Simferopol, I alone appeared, a pathway to the staircase had to be opened up through the horde of locals pressed around it. To accomplish this feat, all the abundant brutality inherent in the attendant Aeroflot air hostesses, all of whom were apparently retired Red Army master sergeants, had to be called upon. Like snarling Dobermans, they would attack the cowering mob, shouting, "Make way for the foreigners!" Then they would punch a pathway through to the stairs, the embarrassed *inastrantsy* (foreigners) all hurrying after, like the Children of Israel double-timing it through the briefly-parted Red Sea.

The most self-conscious I ever felt during one of these episodes was on a miserable winter's day at the Domodedova Airport in Moscow. When the foreigners' bus finally pulled up near the plane, a huge, shivering mob was huddled around the mobile staircase, standing in snow two feet deep, as a blizzard was in progress. From the amount of snow piled up on the people's shoulders and heads, they had been there for quite some time, but they reeled backward like intimidated sheep as the hostess-sergeants bellowed and shoved them out of the way.

Once aloft, passengers could generally look forward to one beverage service by the hostesses, regardless of the length of the flight, and some domestic flights within the USSR – say Moscow to Khabarovsk in the Soviet Far East, near Japan – could seemingly last for days. This one service gave the passenger a choice of apple juice and water mixed half and half, or, if you preferred, straight water. And that was it.

The airline's usual passenger contingent – heavily bundled up and fur-hatted – already knew not to expect any culinary delights courtesy of the airline and came prepared with their own stores of bread, salami, apples, water and vodka. The ones apparently coming from the countryside were better provisioned than the city folk, the latter identifiable by their somewhat snappier attire and the thin, battered briefcases carried by all citified males in the USSR at all times. The country types spent their time eating and drinking – at least until everything was gone – while the urbanites were more likely to pass the time staring at the backs of the heads in front of them.

But there was yet another element to be considered: the cockpit crew. On flights of American air carriers and most others as well, the pilot, copilot and navigator were usually in the cockpit when you boarded the plane and were still there when you exited.

Soviet Union: Flying the funky skies of Aeroflot

Not so with the old Aeroflot domestic flights. The officers were the last to board the plane, reminding me of my days in the U.S. Army when we enlisted men would be herded into a large, bare room and made to sit there, not speaking, until whoever was going to address us arrived. A sergeant would then shout, "A-ten-HUTT!" and we would all leap to our feet like automotons. Well, the Aeroflot passengers didn't leap to their feet, but the feeling was the same. The captain and the other officers, wearing uniforms like Navy dress blues, and huge, twelve-inch-diameter "flying saucer" hats, would enter the plane from the rear and parade up the aisle to the cockpit. I suppose the cleaning lady had already done the pre-flight check, because as best I could tell, the captain just stuck his key in the ignition, started the engines and took off. Of course the flight might already be four hours late in departing, but once the flight crew was on board, you were gone.

After five or six en route stops, depending on the cities of origination and destination, the plane would roll to a stop, its engines would be switched off, and all the passengers would sit meekly in their seats for the thirty seconds or so required for the flight crew to leave the cockpit and parade, stony-faced, back down the aisle and off the plane. Next it was the foreigners' turn, and lest any bumpkin not be aware of this item of protocol, a sergeant-hostess would bellow it out, no P.A. system required. After the exit of the foreigners, the lowly citizens of the USSR were at last free to push and claw their way toward the door.

In all fairness, I should mention that Aeroflot did not have exclusive rights to the system of alternative forms of service as described above. Other airlines of the East Bloc vied mightily to outdo the Soviet carrier in this field, and sometimes succeeded.

I have normally never checked a bag on any flight. Whatever belongings I have taken, I have kept with me in the passenger compartment. An exception to this rule was when, for reasons never explained to me, I was forced to check my small bag before a Czechoslovak Airlines flight from East Berlin to Prague. As soon as my little suitcase disappeared on the conveyor belt into the pit behind the check-in counter, it was apparently fed directly into a garbage truck outfitted with trash compactor, where it was smashed and torn to bits. In Prague, upon reclaiming my pile of ripped, smashed and grease-coated remnants, I was told that the airline couldn't do anything about it. My suitcase must have been defective.

But I must confess that airlines of the other Communist countries could also offer value for money paid. I remember buying a ticket in Sofia, Bulgaria, for a flight on the Bulgarian airline to Gorna Oryakhovitsa, some 130 miles to the east, for the equivalent of $1.34 U.S. In retrospect, I would say it was worth at least twice that, if only for the spooky thrill of being able to look out my window and see a huge, somewhat roundish object which looked like a lopsided black onion – one of the plane's completely bald tires – suspended on struts from the overhead wing, and wondering what the odds were of its surviving the landing.

Ah, well. So much for flying with the comrades.

TRAINS, CARS, BOATS AND . . .

When traveling on my own by train, I always opted for third class in countries which offered it, as in Spain and Portugal, second class otherwise. While second class compartments had six seats, third class had eight, although it was quite common to have ten people squeezed into the compartment. The seats were undesignated – that is, there was simply a bench perhaps twelve to fourteen inches deep, not deep enough to slouch down in, to sleep. On the more important runs, the third class seats would have an inch or so of padding, while the seats on trains making local runs would be of plain wood. In warm or hot weather, the windows would be open.

Trains in the USSR also had classes, which I thought rather odd. The dictatorship of the proletariat, every man an equal, and all that. But they did, Soft Class and Hard Class. Foreigners had no choice: they were required to buy Soft Class tickets and thus lead the soft life, at least by Soviet standards. A little "potato lady" in a white smock attended to a huge samovar at the end of your car and would bring you a glass of steaming sweet tea in a tall glass sitting in a fancy little metal glass holder with a dainty handle. On overnight journeys, men and women were assigned to double compartments without regard to sex. Bashful ladies finding themselves sharing with a Stalin-mustachioed Cossack usually chose to sleep in their clothes, if they could sleep at all, and with a shoe or some other make-do weapon under the covers with them, just in case.

Russian trains on most of the main routes used by foreigners were pulled by big, green-painted diesel engines with a large red star on the engine's "nose." In Western Europe, most main trains were pulled by either diesel or electric engines, although there were still plenty of the old coal-burning locomotives in operation – especially in Spain. There, one might begin an overnight journey from, say, San Sebastián, with the train being pulled out of the station by a respectable-looking, modern enough diesel engine, and wake up with a diesel pulling the train into Madrid's Estación del Norte. What you might not know is that most of the way, the train had been pulled by one of those old smoke-belching steam engines with five-foot smokestacks. Sort of like pouring cheap scotch into the Chivas Regal bottle: it makes a better impression.

Spain offered a cheap little mini-train of sorts. It was called an *automotor,* a self-powered diesel rail car which trundled along some of the country's worst-riding tracks – tracks so buckled and uneven that at times the passengers were repeatedly bouncing a good three inches off their seats. There was nothing you could do to stay on your seat, and sometimes these very rough segments would last a good half minute or so – which could *seem* like several minutes on a bucking bronco. A few passengers, mostly the very young or the very old, would appear frightened, but most of the people just laughed nervously, waiting for the bouncing to let up. The back door of the rail car was usually open, with no protective bar across the gap. I would stand in that doorway and watch the Spanish countryside roll by. Better than being shaken, not stirred, in my seat.

All over Europe, a common sight at railroad crossings would be a wagon or a two-wheeled cart, often laden with hay or vegetables, and pulled by a horse, mule, burro or ox. Sometimes the driver would doff his hat or beret to the train. More than once my train stopped in the middle of nowhere, for some unknown reason, and some shepherd boys, their sheep grazing nearby, would come up to the train and play their flutes for the passengers looking out the open windows. Occasionally a passenger would toss the boys a coin. I requested that the young musicians play Chubby Checker's "The Twist," but they declined; I guess they were tired of playing it.

Roads and highways in Spain were used primarily by trucks and buses, although there were private cars driven by the upper class and, to a lesser degree, by the small middle class. In France and on to the rest of Western Europe, more private cars were to be seen. Hitchhiking could be an iffy thing. Occasionally drivers would stop for you, many times, I think, because they recalled their own days in the not-too-distant past, when they would have appreciated a lift. But most wealthy Spaniards paid hitchhikers no notice.

Many of the secondary roads were unpaved, and during a dry spell this could mean vehicles trailing huge dust clouds. As all vehicle windows were open in fair weather, riding those dusty back roads would mean a grimy face and collar later on, just as with trains and their coal engine soot. Even in many towns, side streets would be unpaved.

But even paved roads could leave much to be desired. Highways designated as "national routes" were still two-lane affairs in most areas, although the Germans did have their Hitler-built autobahns here and there. *All* the roads of Iceland were of dirt; only in downtown Reykjavik were there paved streets.

Driving from Switzerland into Italy via the St. Bernard Pass could be an adventure in the late spring to mid autumn. The rest of the year it wasn't an adventure because the pass was snowed in and closed to automobile traffic. Even in midsummer the snow piled up on each side of the road could be as high as twenty-five feet. All of this was of course before the Great St. Bernard Tunnel from Switzerland to Italy opened in 1964.

Once at the Italian border, drivers would stop and go inside a small building to buy gasoline coupons. Italy offered these coupons to foreigners at a 33% discount off the normal, expensive, gas prices. You used them when you filled up your car's tank later on. Drivers would try to determine how many kilometers they would drive in Italy and, hence, how many liters of gasoline they would need.

Especially in Mediterranean areas, you could often see women washing clothes along the side of a river.

Upon arrival in any Italian – or Spanish – town, one might very well be "serenaded" by a slowly cruising vehicle with a big loudspeaker mounted on its top blaring out the frantic words of a man with a microphone inside the car or truck, usually advertising a circus or some other performance, or else making a pitch for a political candidate in a forthcoming election. When the impassioned announcer ran out of breath, a stint of fuzzy-sounding recorded music went blasting through the streets.

STOP signs on European streets and highways were rather unimaginative, usually black letters on a square white sign saying STOP in the local language: HALT! In Germany, ARRET in France, ALTO in Spain, and so on. Today the U.S.-style sextagonal STOP sign, white letters on on red, is universal.

Most people traveled relatively short distances across water via ferry boat, as opposed to airplane; the ferry was much cheaper. I paid a grand total of $1.70 for third class ferry travel from Barcelona to Palma de Mallorca, an overnight trip. At least on that trip I stayed dry, despite my deck passage. On a ferry boat from Patras, Greece, to Brindisi, Italy, I was not so fortunate. A heavy rain came up shortly after we left port on the overnight journey, and so I and all of my fellow deck passage travelers hurried down some steps, into the hold of the big ferry boat. There was no seating of any kind in the hold, just huge wooden crates of cargo, coils of hawser lines two inches thick, and machinery. The rain increased and poured through a big, open hatch, soon making the deck of the hold a couple of inches deep in water, which rushed to one end of the vessel and then back again, as we pitched through the rough seas. The ferry's Turkish toilet – a "one-holer" – at the stern of the hold eventually flooded, sending its horrors floating out into the waters surging back and forth along the deck of the hold. I found a big coil of wet hawser rope, mounted it and remained there all night, in an effort to escape the "here it comes, there it goes" floating tides with their mines of poop. And even if I could somehow manage to doze off in my squatting position up on the hawser coil, I would be awakened by a Greek Orthodox priest in a black, stovepipe hat, wailing away like a *muezzin* atop his minaret. What a night!

A mechanical device which one might look at suspiciously when the subject of transportation is being discussed is the elevator. The lift. The acensor. I refer to the old "birdcage" variety which prevailed at one time. You would enter the building, proceed to the lift shaft, which looked like something Gustave Eiffel might have built with a big Erector Set, and press the "call" button. Somewhere above you, you would hear a crashing of metal gates, then a humming sound, and you would see through the grillwork of the device the snake-like cables inside the shaft, moving up and down as the passenger cabin descended to your level. Once the contraption clanked into place, you would open the outer, grilled door, then spread apart the collapsible inner grilled gate, enter the car, do everything as before, but in reverse order, and finally press the button for your desired floor or *etage*. With yet another clashing of metal things you would be on your way. Of course, if the elevator had an operator, it was all made easier. When, with the coming of Fidel Castro and the resulting rash of hijackers demanding planes be flown to Cuba, I recall fantasizing about a small band of bearded types in green army fatigues rushing an elevator on the ground floor of an office building and pointing a pistol at the operator, a beard growling the order: "To Havana!"

8

The East Was Red
– Part of It

THE ONLY CHINA FOR AMERICANS: TAIWAN AND HONG KONG

Many people probably don't remember or know that the capital of "Red China" – it was almost never called the People's Republic of China – was Peiping (pronounced "Bay-ping") before it became Peking, and then later, Beijing. Whatever it was called, Americans couldn't go there. The only China U.S. tourists could visit was the island Republic of China, first known as Formosa, later as Taiwan, and commonly referred to then as Nationalist China or Free China. It was the surviving remnant of Chiang Kai Shek's noncommunist government which fled to the island when Mao's forces took over mainland China in 1949, following years of civil war.

I took groups to Taiwan, which, as the Republic of China, was still technically at war with the People's Republic. Warplanes were constantly overhead, as actual war was still going on over the nearby islands of Quemoy and Matsu, still occupied by the Nationalists but coveted by the Reds and shelled by them daily from the mainland a few miles away. Taiwan didn't offer the casual tourist too much to see, really, but, as people said, "It's the only China we've got for tourists." The main attraction was the mind-boggling, classical Chinese style Grand Hotel in Taipei, where my groups stayed. The hotel was a massive place built in traditional Chinese style and painted, most appropriately,

Chinese red (not to be confused with Red Chinese), and had the old green-tiled sort of roof, and gilt paint around the columns, doors and windows. The hotel was owned by Madame Chiang Kai Shek, wife of Nationalist China's president-for-life.

One evening in Taipei I was dining with my group in a large, noisy Chinese restaurant, sitting at a big table with seven other people. A young fellow from the kitchen was going about the room from table to table, showing the diners something in a bucket he was carrying. Finally, he came to our table and let us all peer into his bucket. It was full of writhing snakes, each about three feet long. You could choose your snake, and the chef would cook it for your dinner.

All the people at my table reacted in the same manner, horrified and saying things like "Ewww!" and "Yuck!" I said to them, "Well, you know, they say snake tastes like chicken," but that didn't win over any takers. Just feeling adventurous, I chose a snake, and the white-smocked guy from the kitchen reached into the bucket and pulled out my choice, holding it just behind its head. The serpent wiggled and twisted as the man held it up, a couple of feet off the floor. Then he pulled out a pocket knife and cleanly cut through the snake's skin at its neck, just behind the head. He now put the knife away, grabbed the tail end of the snake and yanked down. The whole skin slid off easily, leaving a live, naked snake writhing more than ever in his grip. The fellow smiled me a toothy smile and went off to the kitchen with his bucket and the naked snake.

Later, I was served my selection, cooked in strips and served atop a pile of rice, prepared much like roasted chicken which had been pulled apart. I ate it, and it wasn't bad.

"What's it like?" everybody asked me. I thought a moment and then replied, "Uh, it tastes like chicken."

HONG KONG: RICKSHA MADNESS

Other than Taiwan, the only other China American tourists could visit was the British Crown Colony of Hong Kong, and all of my tours included this spot. Hong Kong experienced no problems that affected tourism -- until Mao dreamed up his Cultural

Taipei: Choosing the main course

Revolution and the Great Leap Forward. Then, all of a sudden, the communist faction called the Red Guards burst onto the scene, exploding bombs in busy areas and rioting in the streets, with everything directed from Beijing. Mobs of Party faithful waved their copies of Mao's Little Red Book – a compilation of his sayings – and sang the latest Party song, *The East Is Red.*

But, surprisingly enough, tourists continued to come to Hong Kong, perhaps because none were ever hurt or inconvenienced by all the noisy monkeyshines. A *de rigueur* excursion took tourists from the downtown Victoria/ Kowloon area to the colony's border with Red China at Lo Wu, in the New Territories. On a hilltop overlooking the frontier crossing, where British army tanks stood watch, one could see rolling farmland, a narrow road and a border crossing point in the distance. At the crossing, small white structures, one on each side of the border, were visible, these being the control buildings of the British and the Chinese. Otherwise, the broad valley ran for many miles, until distant mountains blocked the way. A creek or small river marked the actual dividing line. A big, empty region.

Contrast that with what one could find decades later in the same spot: an urban setting of hundreds of highrises and even skyscrapers, like Manhattan. This was the Special Economic Zone of Shenzhen, built by the Chinese government just across the border with Hong Kong, an area with more lenient trade rules and regulations, meant to compete with Hong Kong, which was of course still in the hands of the British.

But long before Shenzhen came into being and that entire stretch of countryside was nothing but farmland, I took a photograph of it from the aforementioned hilltop overlook, the one with the British tanks on guard. I had my photos developed into 35mm color slides, and on the slide of the picture just mentioned, I took a red ink marker pen and I colored red the entire area on the far side of the border river. Thus when I showed my slides to any poor sucker who might have been trapped into watching them, my captive audience could clearly see what was meant when one talked about Red China.

By the way, as you might imagine, those British tanks, as well as the U.K. troops scattered about the colony, were purely for show. If China had wanted to overrun the place, it could have easily done so, probably in a matter of minutes. But they found Hong Kong – and the small nearby Portuguese colony of Macao – useful as international trade gateways for the People's Republic. The Red Guard business, the occasional bomb and the street demonstrations, was also merely for show, this time on the part of the Chinese government. Just tweaking the Westerners' big noses.

On my first visit to Hong Kong I was introduced to an amazing sound. I was in the hotel where my group was staying and I was headed for the dining room, when I heard this godawful, high-pitched screeching noise. It sounded like big sheets of metal being dragged against each other, and it was coming from my goal: the dining room. When I entered, I immediately discovered the source. Up on a stage at one end of the room, a classical Chinese orchestra was playing.

In Hong Kong and in other Asian cities of the time, rickshas were still in vogue, serving as taxis. They were one-seaters pulled by barefoot coolies, and they were not expensive. It became popular for some members of my groups to engage two or more such two-wheeled conveyances and have ricksha races, say from a restaurant where we had just eaten, to our hotel a few blocks away. The winning coolie would receive a bonus, over his fee. A good time was had by all – except the coolies, I imagine.

MACAO: A LITTLE PIECE OF PORTUGAL IN THE FAR EAST

I mentioned Portuguese Macao. This colony, occupying a much smaller area than Hong Kong, was forty minutes away by hydrofoil and was a very popular day excursion destination for tourists in Hong Kong. It was also very popular with many of the Hong Kong Chinese, who now went there regularly to gamble in the new casino down by the waterfront. There were no casinos in Hong Kong.

Macao then looked like a good-sized little Portuguese town. Its white, arcaded buildings with red tiled roofs could have been lifted right out of Portugal. Today, Macao, like Shenzhen, looks like Manhattan. There was one garish modern edifice, the Lisboa Casino on the waterfront, the only such gambling palace in the Far East at the time. Inside, the look was Las Vegas, only a little seedier.

Mao's Cultural Revolution had reached Macao, too. There were even full-sized billboards showing caricatured Westerners with exaggerated long noses cowering in the presence of red-starred Chinese communist hero-giants who were putting to flight the running dogs of Capitalism. The Portuguese colonial government apparently couldn't or wouldn't bring itself to say or do anything about such propaganda. Like Hong Kong, Macao lived at China's tolerance.

Down by the port side of the peninsula where the broad Pearl River flowed southward from Canton (now Gwangzhou), Portuguese style buildings took on a more Chinese air, with calligraphy signs painted on whitewashed walls. In the side streets, little Chinese kids and old granny types sat crosslegged in the dirt, making firecrackers to be sold later. Macao was the fireworks-producing center of Asia. At the border with China, heavy Chinese army-type trucks rumbled through the triumphal arch marking the frontier. No automobile traffic seemed to be headed in or out of the People's Republic.

There were a few Portuguese army troops in evidence throughout the small colony, but I suspect each man had a white flag tucked away under his shirt, just in case the People's Army suddenly showed up from across the border.

The first western-style casino, the Lisboa, had just recently opened, and it was an immediate hit with many of the Hong Kong Chinese, for whom gambling is a way of life, and this Las Vegas-style emporium was most welcome. (Note: There are 33 casinos in Macao today). There were roulette, slots, craps, poker, etc. I went in to take a looksee, observing the packed tables and taking in the frantic atmosphere. Before leaving, I decided to use the casino's toilet facilities, because I knew they had to be better than what I would find elsewhere.

On entering the mens' room, I found myself in a circular sort of place, with perhaps eight or ten toilet stalls facing inward. All of them showed the red "occupied" sign by the door handle. Apparently a lot of poker players were taking a break at the same time. The bathroom attendant, an elderly Chinese man wearing a white smock and guarding the tips basket by the exit, saw me checking out the stall doors. Flashing me an incredibly toothy smile, seemingly revealing hundreds of brightly polished choppers, he happily crowed, "Full house!"

WALKING THE STRAIGHT AND
NARROW IN SINGAPORE

The island city-nation of Singapore became a self-governing state within the British Commonwealth in 1959, and independent in 1963. It is small, not thirty miles across at its widest point, but what it lacks in size it has made up for in laws. Just prior to landing at Singapore's Changi Airport, a lovely young Asian flight hostess would demurely murmur over the aircraft's P.A. system, "All persons arriving in Singapore are reminded that the penalty for drug-trafficking in Singapore is death. Have a nice stay in Singapore, ladies and gentlemen."

The two gum-chewing American teenagers sitting across the aisle from me got a good laugh out of the attendant's announcement, their hippy-length hair flouncing about as they animatedly joked with each other about smuggling pot into Singapore. Rich daddies, I figured.

I had read in the Singapore news about three men from another Asian country who were caught smuggling in a large quantity of heroin. Singaporeans just wagged their heads at the utter stupidity of the act, for there was absolutely no doubt whatsoever as to the drug smugglers' fate: the gibbet. And there would be no chance for appeal.

On an earlier trip, I read about someone else being sentenced to death by a Singapore court, but not for a drug offense. This particular crime involved sodomy, and the lawyer for the defendant was quite clearly facing an uphill battle, as his client was admittedly guilty. The attorneys' only tack was to argue that in some other, more enlightened countries, one had the right to do such things, as long as consenting adults were involved.

The court's patient response was that Singaporean law did not infringe on anyone's right to normal sex, as long as a legally married man and woman were in mutual agreement

121

on the matter, and as long as the acceptable position was utilized for the acceptable act. Nobody had any problem with that. But sodomy? Unh-unh.

Previous comments notwithstanding, however, I liked Singapore. It was pleasant and clean. There was no litter on the streets, and the buildings were in good shape. The cars were good and shiny, too. There were no old clunkers, as there was a law which said no car which was dirty, dented, or more than seven years old could be operated in Singapore. By the end of the seventh year, the family jalopy got packed off to Malaysia or Indonesia, or some other less fastidious country. You didn't see any graffiti in Singapore, either. It was well known that it was a serious crime to paint on walls, poles, tree trunks, or cars, or to otherwise deface them. As one young American could recently confirm, the penalty was a stiff caning with a split bamboo pole.

But there were, besides drug trafficking, sodomy, and graffiti painting, other crimes to be on guard against in Singapore.

Does it bug you when you go to use a public toilet and find that the previous user didn't bother to flush it? Well, in Singapore, if you knew who didn't flush, you could run to the nearest cop, point out the culprit, and the law would take its course. I wondered what the penalty was for Failing to Flush Public Toilet. I could never find that out, and I wasn't sure I wanted to know.

Chinese people have always been renowned as the world's most prolific hawkers-and-spitters, so with about eighty percent of Singapore's population being ethnic Chinese the no-spitting law must have been a tough one for the locals to swallow. There were also laws against feeding birds, picking flowers, jaywalking and public urinating.

And how about gum? Don't you just hate to step on a sticky blob of chewing gum

Singapore: Walking the straight and narrow

some cretin spat onto the sidewalk, or worse, left on a park bench or theatre seat for you to sit on? Well, it almost assuredly wouldn't happen to you in Singapore, because chewing gum was illegal. Frankly, I thought this was the best of all their laws. I wouldn't mind having it in America.

I was brought back to the present by the plane touching down. We taxied to Changi Airport's terminal. Once inside, I heard some loud voices speaking English with American accents, in argumentative tones.

I looked and saw, up ahead of me, the two teenagers from the plane. They were no longer chewing gum, and they were being firmly escorted by two uniformed Singaporean policemen toward a special barber shop, where a smiling Chinese barber waited in the doorway.

I forgot to mention earlier that long hair on men was also illegal in Singapore, and lawbreakers had no choice but to purchase an expensive buzz cut upon arrival.

I had no doubt but what the Singaporean authorities would have heartily endorsed the quotation, "Good laws have their origins in bad morals." But then I didn't suppose the man who said that, Albert Einstein, ever visited Singapore. Not with *his* hairdo.

THE SOUTH PACIFIC

These last four items do not really deal with Asia, per se, but I couldn't think of any other place to insert them. One of them involves a place that was in Papeete, Tahiti. I say was, because it is long gone now. But while it still existed, Quinn's Bar in Papeete was the stuff of tales of the South Pacific going way back. It was variously described as The Toughest Bar in the World and The Worst Bar in the World.

For many years authors like Maugham, Michener and others regaled the reading world with stories about Quinn's Bar. It was the place every seafaring adventurer worth his salt headed for, upon arriving in Tahiti. Legends centered around Quinn's abounded. So, naturally, the first time I found myself in Papeete, I headed for Quinn's.

I was not disappointed. It was as sleazy and colorful as I had hoped. Quinn's was in a ramshackle wooden building with a corregated iron roof, located a couple of blocks down the waterfront from the town's main street running inland. Outside, above the front door, QUINN'S BAR was spelled out in bamboo letters. Inside, it was pretty dark, because the only daylight came through the two doors at the front. There was a long bar which ran between the two doors, and then there were crude wooden booths along the walls. In the center of the room were a few very beat-up tables and chairs. In fact, everything in the place (all of it was made of wood) was very battered and very carved up. All surfaces seemed to have names, hearts, dates, etc., carved into them. And the patrons of the place couldn't have been more appropriate if Central Casting from Hollywood had picked them: drunk sailors, grubby planter types, a French Foreign Legionnaire, a tough-looking bouncer, and hookers galore. The air was thick with smoke and the smell of liquor. The toilet was a single, unisex cubicle separated from the rest of the place only by a dirty curtain. Cockroaches covered the floor.

I bellied up to the bar and ordered a beer. While sipping it, I was approached by two separate ladies, each apparently wanting to sell me something. But then I became aware of some kind of altercation in the back of the room. A rough-visaged man was dragging a rather bedraggled-looking Polynesian woman wearing a flowered muumuu toward the door, but she was protesting in some language, maybe

Polynesian. If it was French, I couldn't catch it. She didn't want to go, and she fought against the man, finally spitting in his face. The ruffian then cold-cocked her with a fist to the side of her head, and she slumped against him. He threw her over his shoulder and went out the door with her. Everybody laughed. I finished my beer and left legendary Quinn's Bar.

DOWN AND DIRTY DOWN UNDER

I was in an upscale book shop in Sydney, Australia, when it was raided by the local police. Several officers fanned out, obviously looking for something specific. At last one of them found what they were looking for; he shouted and proudly held up an unrolled poster maybe 24" x 30", a black and white photo of Michelangelo's statue of David, full frontal and all: pornography!

After a long session between the head cop and the store manager, the policeman left with all the cardboard tubes containing the David poster. Just one more step in the civic effort to spare Sydney the ignominy of imported filth from abroad. I breathed a sigh of relief.

I felt safer now.

DESPERATE DECEPTION IN NEW CALEDONIA

I had a group in Noumea, French New Caledonia, and it was here that I designed and carried out The Great Evasion. The hotel in Noumea which had been booked by my company was, uncharacteristically, a dump of the first water. Not only was it shabby and not so clean, the guest room beds actually had bedbugs. Mercifully, our stay there was for but a night, a stopover break between Fiji and Australia. But this was long enough for

Sydney: The great porno raid!

my group members to howl with complaints. Now, I knew something they didn't, and that was that there was a much higher rated hotel, a resort type of property constructed in the modern style, and that it was located on the coast road, en route to what little areas of interest there were to see on the island. If we drove past it on our sightseeing tour, my very head would be in danger. Bad as our hotel was, the group members thought it was the best of a bad lot; I had to keep them thinking that way.

I asked our local tour people if there wasn't *some* road, *any* road we could take on our only tour of the island, to drive up Mt. Koghi and to see the barrier reef, without driving past the good hotel. Everybody said no, the coast road was it. Then one old fellow said that actually, there *was* another road, but it was dirt, rutted, and just plain bad. Very bad. We took it. Most of the people complained loudly, but, mercifully, a few innocent souls interjected that, after all, we were on a backwater French colonial island in the wide expanse of the South Pacific; what more could one expect? Yes! Yes! I shouted to myself upon hearing these reasoned arguments. Yes!

Later, at the airport prior to departure for Sydney, I learned that the water at the deluxe hotel had been shut off for work on the pipes for *a full hour* the day before, and the Americans who had been staying there were still furious, making it sound like they had *never* had running water. On hearing those complaining people, one man in my group came up to me and said, "Well, our hotel wasn't much, but at least we had a better one than those people in that other group."

Yes! I screamed silently.

9

Potty Talk

POTTY TALK

The U.S. led the world in all things bathroom-related back then. In the majority of hostelries I frequented, the most I could expect in the way of hygienic devices was a sink in the room (which, nevertheless, could come in handy in the middle of the night), but most often it was simply a wash stand and a pitcher of water. The bowl would usually be made of galvanized iron, sometimes with an enameled coating (usually chipped). The bathroom would be down the hall, and you prayed it would not be locked, with some prima donna guest languishing in a long tub bath. It was not uncommon for guests in a hurry to hammer on a locked bathroom door with a fist. Whether that did any good or not is another matter.

Toilet paper seemed to come in one of three forms: slick, waxed-paper-like stuff, most popular in Britain, and which defied logic; gray or beige-colored rolls of crepe paper, which reminded one of the old term, "rough as a cob"; and, lastly, approximately 6 x 9-inch squares of newsprint, torn by hand from old newspapers, usually hung on a nail.

The toilets themselves tended to be ancient contraptions with the water tank located high up on the wall above, with a long chain to flush it with. The nauseating smell of sewer gas was very common, particularly in the older buildings.

My first time use of a public toilet on the continent (Brussels, I think) introduced me to the European practice of cleaning women working in the men's toilets without closing off the facility. Some first-time American visitors were too abashed to stay, and retreated – until the working ladies finished their tasks. Personally, I just fell back on that old philosophical viewpoint: *If she's seen it before . . .*

Those public toilets could be real horror shows, especially as one traveled south. In Mediterranean lands, the Turkish toilet, or "one-holer", was quite common: a single hole in a tiled floor, with two slightly raised footpads flanking it – and no flushing involved. I remember going into the men's room (with one-holers only) in Barcelona's Estación de Francia, whose windows were so soot-begrimed as to be opaque, and using the bathroom facilities there; a large and most unusual hunk of human excrement lay just to the side of the gaping hole of my selected toilet, as its producer had obviously missed his mark. Well, one month later, at that same one-holer, the aforementioned bizarre turd was *still there.*

HONEYMOON AT A "ONE-HOLER"

On our "shoestring honeymoon" to Europe, my bride and I stopped to gas up our rental VW at a filling station in northern Italy. I pointed out the ladies' room to her, and she proceeded to her destination while I saw to getting the car refueled. In just a moment she came running out, calling my name, a worried expression on her face.

"That's the men's room!" she cried, upset and pointing at the women's toilet.

I knew that many Americans had trouble differentiating the the Italian words for "gentlemen" and "ladies", as they were very similar: *signori* and *signore*, but I could clearly see *signore* posted over the ladies'. But who knew? Maybe -- Well, best to simply take a look. I walked over to the little cubicle in question, my wife right behind me, and I poked my head in the door.

Inside, I saw a rather grubby Turkish "one-holer", actually good for women *or* men. My wife had never seen such a toilet before, and simply didn't understand. I assured her that this was the right place, and she reluctantly went on in. But she didn't like it, and she has never liked "one-holers" encountered elsewhere (usually in remote areas of Africa or Asia) ever since, either.

Russian toilets featured a commode, or potty, but they were the filthiest of all. A sign in Russian (and maybe in English) ordered the user to deposit all toilet paper into a wire trash basket or cardboard box off to the side. If you tried to flush the paper down the toilet, it would almost assuredly back up and pour the now-yucky water all over the floor. Even if you put no paper in the toilet, chances are the thing would not flush anyway. You would just pull the chain and – *thunk*. Nothing. But you probably gathered that would be the case when you first entered the toilet stall: evidence of previous guests.

Toilets on trains usually functioned properly, if only because the process was very simple: a foot pedal on the floor triggered the opening of a metal flap at the bottom of the pot, and then gravity did the rest, depositing everything onto the crossties of the track below, as the train rumbled on. Hence the reason for the conductor locking the toilets when the train pulled into a station, then unlocking them on departure. This whole procedure was in common with the rules for train toilet use in the U.S. when I was younger, and was the inspiration behind a then-popular ditty, sung to the tune of *Humoresque:*

Men and women please refrain
From flushing toilets while the train

Is standing in the station, we thank you!
We encourage constipation while the train is in the station,
When the train is moving, so may you!

I once had a group flying from Budapest to Prague in an old, prop-driven, Russian Tupelov. Emigration had been maddeningly slow, and we had to rush to make it aboard the flight. In fact, as the last person in my group made it onto the plane, the door was shut. One man, Mr. Cohen, had a hanging suit bag which he tried to give to a flight hostess, to hang someplace, but the crew was too busy readying the aircraft for departure, so he just sat in his seat, with his suit bag in his lap. After we reached cruising altitude, Mr. Cohen got up from his seat and carried his suit bag toward the rear of the plane, where he had seen a curtain, which he figured was the coat closet. When he whipped open the curtain, a large Hungarian lady sitting on the pot shouted at him, and he immediately closed the curtain and returned to his seat. He sat the rest of the flight with his hanging bag in his lap.

I had a bothersome toilet experience in London one time. I went down the steps to the Gentlemen's Loo in Leicester Square and encountered lines of men waiting at the three urinals. The line in the center was by far the shortest, so I of course joined that one. But I soon realized that while the lines on either side of me were moving, my line was not – at least not until someone in the line in front of me gave up and left for one of the two other lines. Finally the last man waiting in front of me similarly left our line, making me next. After a minute or so, I realized that the fellow at the urinal in front of me, a short young man, wasn't doing anything – except peering down from side to side at the nether regions of the gentlemen flanking him at the other two urinals. Checking things out, it seemed. With a sigh, I, too, left the center line and joined one of the other two.

The sidewalk *pissoirs* of Paris were great places for *boulevardiers* who wished to pause for a moment. On many streets in downtown Paris one could find a *pissoir*, a round, cast iron structure on the sidewalk, a place where men could relieve themselves at their leisure. The circular, metal walls began about two feet from the ground and went about three feet up, meaning the users' lower legs and head and shoulders were clearly visible throughout the operation. What a handy stopping place, although admittedly *un peu* odoriferous. Unfortunately, the *pissoirs* of Paree, which first appeared in 1841, were eventually decided to be no-nos, and their removal was begun in the 1960s. (Only one such urinal is left today, located just outside Paris's largest penal institution, La Santé Prison.)

Up to now I have mentioned toilets, but not sewers. By far the most bizarre sewer I ever came across in a capital city was in Belize City, in the then British Honduras (now Belize). There was virtually no tourism to the place back then, and only one decent hotel – and it was not a beach hotel, although there were nice beaches nearby. The town had one main street, flanked by dilapidated wooden buildings stewing in the steamy, tropical sun, and down the very center of that street was an open sewer that would make one gag to look at it, much less smell it – which could be done from two blocks away.

My first hotel room with its own private bathroom was in Lucerne, Switzerland. And everything worked. It was so wonderful I felt like I'd died and gone to heaven.

A last item in this fecalo-urinalogical section is perhaps a bit off the mark, but where else to put it? I refer to a feature I found early on in the men's room at the Hofbrauhaus and other big German beer halls (I can't say if such was to be found in the ladies', as my investigations did not go that far).

Just inside the entrance to the spacious gentlemen's toilet, one could observe a sort of nasty concrete pit a few feet deep and perhaps eight feet wide, with a black, iron railing meant for leaning on, while one barfed up the liters of beer recently consumed in the great *Bierhalle*, thus readying oneself for a renewed go, Roman style. A vomitorium, if you will. You didn't want to look down into the pit. Lovely. Many years later, the pit was replaced by a gleaming stainless steel basin, self flushing.

Egad. Let us move on to another subject.

10

South of the Border

I SAW SUPERMAN IN CUBA

Ask any Cuban male who was a teenager or older when Castro took over who Superman was, and I guarantee you he will smile. Everybody knew Superman. Not personally, maybe, but they knew who he was and why he was famous.

I saw Superman in 1955 on a trip to Havana with some friends, a natural prolongation of a party trip to Florida. We were youngsters on our first real fling in the Big, Bad World, and we loved every minute of it. Nothing was illegal in Cuba. Everything was for sale. Openly. My mind reels, just thinking about it.

An American sailor told us, "You gotta see Superman. If you leave Havana without seeing Superman, you'll never forgive yourselves!" So we went to see Superman. He performed at what I thought at the time was a pretty swanky place, along with another headliner, Miss Wonderly; Superman and Miss Wonderly, the Dynamic Duo of Havana. Only they performed separately, not together.

After a bunch of striptease "warmup" acts in the hot, smoky joint which served as a theater, Miss Wonderly came onstage. She was a sort of Jayne Mansfield type, a big, bleached blonde mamoo with humongous bazooms – in the days before silicone implants. The band played sultry music as she strutted around clad in a clinging white silk dress which she finally (finally!) removed, raising among other things the temperature in the room considerably. Miss

Wonderly eventually slinked offstage amidst thunderous applause and howls from the male portion of the audience.

Now it was Superman's turn. I guess he had been watching Miss Wonderly from backstage, because he came out, er, *ready*. No insecure man should ever have gone to see Superman, because it was inevitable that he would see himself as a failure forever

Havana: Watching Superman perform

afterward. Superman didn't just surpass one's own attributes – he *doubled* them. (Maybe even tripled them, depending on who you were.)

The star of the show, the fortyish Afro-Cuban with a Charles Atlas physique to go with his outstanding attraction – you could truly say this was a star-studded performance – was joined by a pretty Conchita Banana type in a tiny negligée and very high heels. She amost immediately removed the negligee, but not the shoes. She wasn't Miss Wonderly, but she was no reject, either. And then she and Superman commenced the real show, part of which involved Superman seated on a kitchen chair. Whew! Even after all those intervening decades, I still break out in a sweat just conjuring up the scene. The women in the audience were hypnotized like deer caught in headlights; men were either laughing nervously or trying to act nonchalant. Me, I was envious as hell.

And that was it. The show was over. I left the theater and reentered the sultry night air of Havana, with the cars blowing their horns, the ladies offering their services, and peddlers selling things from trays suspended from their necks by straps. Oh, man, I thought: Up, up and awaaaaaaaay!

ARGENTINA: SUDDENLY IT'S 1940

I had always heard that Buenos Aires was a great city, but that when you visited there, it was a case of "suddenly it's 1940", meaning that everything was behind the times, *vis a vis* the U.S. The funny thing is that it was "still 1940" there as late as the 1980s. My first time there was in 1959, and the *porteños*, the people of Buenos Aires, or "B.A.", were full of contempt for the new traffic light which had been installed at a busy downtown intersection. I made a point of seeking it out, and there it was, the light systematically changing from green to yellow to red, and back to green. The only problem was that nobody paid any attention to it. Cars zoomed through the red light as though the device were not there. I asked a policeman on the beat about the totally ignored light, and he replied, "Oh, that is simply some gadget the city got from the *yanquis*. Nobody wants it. Nobody pays it any attention." Well, that was obvious.

And speaking of traffic, there was a considerable amount on B.A.'s huge 9th of July Avenue, said to be the widest street in the world. I was surprised to see a goodly number of two-wheeled carts, pulled by mules and burros, mixed in with those speeding cars and taxis. On the subject of taxis, they were virtually all black 1939 Chevrolets. It seems that there was a national import duty of 100% on imported automobiles less than twenty years old. And Argentina made no cars of its own at that time. Since this was 1959, all the taxis were 1939 models, or older. But most were "new" '39 Chevvies.

I walked to one of Buenos Aires's leading deluxe hotels, one near to where I was staying in a considerably more modest place. At the portico entrance, the hotel doorman was giving the old straightarmed, fascist salute to a policemen who was walking by. I didn't know whether the fellow was just goofing off, or being serious. I went on inside the hotel, which was extremely luxurious in the Old European style. Curious, I mounted the wide, plush-carpet-covered staircase to the mezzanine, where the big meeting rooms were, and I walked down the broad passage, marveling at the sparkling chandeliers and the red velvet draperies. At the end of the hallway I peered through a cracked doorway into a banqueting room which was being set up by hotel workers. Hanging from the far wall were three floor-to-ceiling swastika banners, bright red with the Nazi cross in a circle halfway down the banner. Wow, I thought: the cheapo U.S. magazines such as the *Police Gazzette* were always coming out with headlines such as, *Hitler Alive in South America*, and the like. Well, I didn't know about Hitler, but his buddies were apparently here.

A SHOT IN THE DARK

My first entry into Peru was at the Lima airport, a late evening arrival aboard a Panagra (Pan American-Grace Airways) DC-8. Before we even reached the immigration counters, I and my fellow passengers lined up at the Health Inspection desk. Everyone in front of me was removing coats and jackets, if any, and rolling up longsleeved shirts or blouses, preparatory to receiving the obligatory smallpox shot on arrival. As I had, as always, my international smallpox vaccination certificate with my passport, and as it was up to date, I reasoned I wouldn't have to have the shot. *Wronnnnnnnng!*

Each and every person in line in front of me was injected, without objection, but when it was my turn at the needle-laden desk, I held up my yellow vaccination certificate, which was required for all foreign travel, and in Spanish I said something to the white-coated attendant about not needing to be vaccinated, since . . .

"Enrolle su manga, por favor!" ("Roll up your sleeve, please!") was the man's reply, and before I knew it, I had been jabbed with the needle. *"Próximo!"* ("Next!") called out the white-coated medico. So much for my vaccination certificate, I thought. I just hoped the guy had used a new needle on me.

THE HIGH YUM MYSTERY

From my table near the waiters' station in the dining room of Lima's Gran Hotel Bolivar, I overheard two waiters frantically discussing what the foreign *turista* was trying to order for breakfast in addition to eggs and toast. It seemed their limited English vocabularies did not include the term High Yum.

The woman's waiter tried telling her they were fresh out of High Yum, but I heard her huffily reply in a syrupy Georgia accent that she could see High Yum being served to others right at that very moment. Being a Georgian myself, I knew that High Yum was of course Southernese for "ham," and the lady herself finally realized what the problem was and managed to make the waiter understand. In fact, when comprehension did at last break across the man's face, the lady began to see the humorous side of the situation and tried to explain to the waiter that the way she pronounced "ham" was "different from the way the Yankees say it."

A few minutes later, I heard the same waiter explaining things to his coworker in Spanish. "The *turista* is of course a foreigner," he said. "I do not know where she is from, but she is not a *yanqui* – she said so herself. Whatever country she is from, and whatever her language, which is somewhat similar to English, the word for *jamón* is High Yum."

PISCO SOURS TO THE RESCUE

It came time for my small group to depart Iquitos, Peru's major port on the Amazon. We were headed back to Lima after staying three days at a rustic, really rather primitive, lodge on the river. I wasn't unhappy to be leaving our bare, cement-floored, thatched-

Lima: The High Yum mystery

roof huts, which contained only two iron cots with mosquito nets, while the generator-produced electricity operated a ceiling fan and a single twenty-five-watt light bulb, during certain hours only.

We had spent our time in the Amazon Basin on jungle treks, our young guide Luis pointing out such sights as tarantulas, tiny orange-splotched poison frogs, huge neon-blue morpho butterflies, and jungle-green snakes ten feet long. We also ventured out onto the great river in hand-paddled boats, going up a backwater to a small Indian village, where the locals wore almost nothing more than homemade necklaces. I knew that this was the real thing, too, not some hokey "native village" set up for tourists, as there were no souvenirs for sale, unless you counted the monkey skulls on bead chains some of the more enterprising Indians tried to swap for baseball caps or teeshirts. Primitive villages like this are long gone now, at least this close to civilization.

When it was time to move on from the Amazon to Lima, we traveled from our river lodge to Iquitos by means of a good-sized motorized boat. From the rickety old pier in Iquitos, our transportation to the small airport was via an open-sided bus. The body of the vehicle was built of pure mahogany atop a standard flatbed truck frame, as mahogany is said to be the only wood in those parts hard enough to withstand the termites which so proliferate, while a metal body can rust through in two or three years in the terrific humidity.

Well, all was fine until we arrived at the Iquitos airport, and the participants in my group began climbing down from our sweltering, termite-proof conveyance.

In the course of this debarkation, a rather hefty lady named Mrs. Woodall alighted from the unusually high step of the bus and, misjudging the distance to the pavement, stepped down hard, her foot striking the pavement at an angle. I clearly heard the crack from ten feet away as her right ankle broke. She screamed in pain and I rushed to her side, frantic with concern. Mr. Woodall stepped from the bus behind her and supported his wife.

"It's broken," Mrs. Woodall cried. "I know it is."

My mind raced. What to do? I blubbered the first thing to come into my mind.

"We'd better get her to the hospital," I said to her dumbstruck husband.

"Not in this godforsaken hellhole!" Mrs. Woodall bellowed. She gasped for breath, then said, "Oh, no. I'm going to Lima. I'm not gonna be stuck in some Amazon witch doctor's shack for weeks while the rest of you fly out of here. Oh, no. Get me on that plane!"

She thinks fast for a foreigner with a broken ankle in the Amazon, I thought to myself, at the same time acknowledging that she was assuredly correct in her initial instinct. Trying to seek proper medical care in Iquitos would be of questionable judgment, especially as there was nothing more than a rather primitive clinic there. But a highly respected Anglo-American hospital was located in Lima, only an hour or so away by air.

"Just get me on that plane to Lima," Mrs. Woodall wailed. "And step on it!" Then she howled, perhaps at the very thought of stepping on anything with her broken foot.

The other members of the group, all demonstrating empathy for the stricken Mrs. Woodall, walked to the aircraft, while Mr. Woodall, two local boys and I carried the agonizing woman to the old Fawcett Airlines DC-4.

Once inside, we found toward the front of the fuselage a set of two seats facing forward, and, just opposite, another set of two seats facing backward. We sat Mrs. Woodall down, and with the help of the flight crew, used several pillows to prop her already-swelling foot and ankle up onto the opposite seat. She groaned and tears ran down her cheeks.

The captain, aware of the situation, assured me that he would radio ahead to Lima and have an ambulance waiting to take Mrs. Woodall to the Anglo-American Hospital the moment we landed. In the meantime, Mrs. Woodall alternately moaned, gasped, and cried out.

"She needs a pain killer," said Mr. Woodall, frantic for his suffering spouse.

He was right, but this was no airborne hospital. The strongest medicine aboard was probably aspirin, if they even had that. And then I had a thought: *booze.* During the Civil War, didn't they liquor up soldiers before sawing off their legs in the absence of anesthetics? The most popular drink for tourists in Peru has always been the pisco sour, sort of the local margarita, and any Peruvian airline would surely have the necessary ingredients aboard. I knew Mrs. Woodall liked pisco sours, so I asked a concerned stewardess to bring us several.

Now, the DC-4 was an unpressurized aircraft, and as we had to fly over some high Andes mountains en route to Lima, it meant that we had to breathe oxygen from those little masks-with-tube-things that drop down from overhead. Thus all of us, Mrs. Woodall included, had to use the masks. She would take a gulp of pisco sour, moan, then take a whiff of oxygen. Then back to her latest pisco sour.

Before too long, Mrs. Woodall's groans were intermixed with giggles and coos, and we kept pouring the pisco sours down her at a therapeutic pace. By the time we arrived

Iquitos: Pisco sours to the rescue

in Lima, with the promised ambulance standing by, Mrs. Woodall was the life of the party. She cackled, giggled and guffawed at everything being said around her.

As the paramedics carried her away, I heard her sing, "Merry Chrishmus t'all, and t'all, a g'night!" And it was March.

THE CUZCO HEATER

Electric heaters often remind me of a short, heavyset group participant in Cuzco, Peru, 11,000 feet up in the Andes, who was constantly complaining of being cold. I should explain that the best hotel in town at that time was a rambling old hulk of a place with no central heating and drafty rooms filled with furniture which appeared to have been crudely made and painted by children. Still, it was the best place available in Cuzco at the time.

Anyway, the gentleman in question asked me to secure a heater for his single hotel room, but while I did my best to comply with his request, I finally had to tell him that there were simply no heaters to be had in Cuzco. Things just weren't that advanced here.

Sometime later, this gentleman stormed into the dining room where I and the rest of the group were seated, ready for dinner. He came straight to me and loudly explained that his most recent of many heater-related discussions with the front desk had resulted in the suggestion that he warm up by climbing into bed, advice which he had finally decided to accept.

"And you know what happened?" he shouted, quite red of face. "Some sumbitch put a hot brick in my bed and I burned my goddamned ass on it!"

Cuzco: The Cuzco heater

GATOR EYES

All places change over the decades – well, almost all do – meaning that often times a person working with tourist groups, like me, has to update his "things we can do" list. One fun event that is no more is the nighttime alligator hunt we would do in Manaus, Brazil, 1000 miles up the Amazon, at the meeting of the two mighty rivers, the Amazon and the Rio Negro (so called because it is the color of Coca-Cola, white the Amazon is a brownish green). After a group dinner we would depart our hotel on the Rio Negro in long, canopied, eighteen-seat canoes with small, quiet outboard motors, and in each a local boy in the prow, who held a powerful flashlight.

After cruising for a while up the river, the flashlight beam would inevitably pick out two close-together red eyes at water level, eyes like tiny red lights. Only the baby gators seemed interested in approaching the light; I suppose the mamas and the daddies knew better. When one of the young alligators came close enough to the canoe, the local boy would reach down and grab it by its neck, hauling it out of the stygian waters and then holding it up for all to see. The little reptiles, usually two to three feet long, did not writhe or struggle at all; they just hung there, limp as a dishrag, as my mother used to say.

Most group members wanted to take flash photographs, and a few brave souls would hold the baby gator by the neck, themselves. Usually, two or three of the ladies would shriek and try to hide behind a husband or a friend. After a few minutes, the boy would throw the gator back into the river, and then we would hunt for another one. After three or four such captures, we would move on to an island in the river, where a big bonfire was burning, a samba band was playing, and caipirinhas were waiting. That was a great evening event.

ACAPULCO AND JOHN WAYNE'S HOUSE

Acapulco was a popular destination at the time. Many years later it would be eclipsed by Cancun and other Mexican resorts, but for now "Alky-pulque" was number one. And one of the top attractions for foreign visitors was the daily Sunset Cruise, with passengers enjoying margaritas while a mariachi band played.

The first part of the cruise was in daylight, while the return to port was after the sun went down. During this earlier part, the cruise boat would pass along an area of cliffs, on the tops of which were built some beautiful homes. One house in particular stood out from all the rest, a huge, ultra-modern mansion which jutted out over the cliff, overlooking the blue Pacific. The first time I took the cruise, the man doing the commentary over the boat's P-A system in Spanish and English drew special attention to this house. "On your right," he said, "the big house on the clifftop belongs to the famous Hollywood star, Rock Hudson." The next time I went, the man said the house belonged to Elizabeth Taylor. And the time after that, it was John Wayne's house. And so on. I quickly determined that "the owner" of that house was whoever was the top movie star of the moment. A Mexican friend told me that the house had been the property of a wealthy Mexican businessman for many years. But all that star stuff sounded great, and the people would enthuse, "Ooooooh! John Wayne!" and rush to the rail for photographs.

By the way, I also heard that same sort of spiel recited by guides in London, Rome, the Caribbean, the French

Riviera, and on and on, *ad nauseum.* Those Hollywood stars really bought a lot of houses.

DOGGEDLY EXPERIENCING HAITI

In the 1950s and '60s, Port-au-Prince, Haiti's capital, was a regular port of call for many cruise ships, while tourists arriving by air usually stayed in the delightful old Victorian gingerbread hotels of Petionville, the exclusive hilltop community located several miles outside of the city on the slopes of Mt. Kenscoff, where cooling breezes tempered the tropical heat.

The arts and crafts hawked by the locals – woodcarvings, paintings, woven items – were well made and sold for a tiny fraction of what they would have cost back in the U.S. It was in this commercial and festive atmosphere that my young wife and I ventured into downtown Port-au-Prince one day.

Estelle was bent on a serious search for local goodies, but after walking half a block in the terrific heat and humidity of the town, I wanted only to find an air conditioned bar and a cold Heineken. It was thus with agreement that we parted near Port-au-Prince's main intersection, deciding that we would meet later at the art gallery on the corner.

At the appointed time, I strolled down the bustling sidewalk toward the gallery and noticed that some sort of disturbance was taking place half a block away. A crowd was in the street at that main intersection, completely blocking traffic in all four directions, and people were yelling and jumping. All their attention seemed directed at someone or something in the very center of the crossroads. I went in the art gallery, but my wife wasn't there, so I went back outside and ventured over to the edge of the crowd in the street, curious as to what might be going on. Standing on tiptoes,

I saw in the very vortex of this seething mass the familiar round, black hairdo of my wife.

Frantic, I pushed my way to the center of the mob, where, in an open circle perhaps thirty feet in diameter, stood a pensive Estelle. She was surrounded by several hand-woven straw rugs spread out on the potholed pavement, and five yelling Haitians, obviously salesmen of the displayed merchandise. Down the traffic-stalled street to the right, I could see two more locals hurrying toward us as fast as they could run while carrying big, rolled-up straw rugs to show to the tourist lady. I groaned.

I burst into the rug-covered center of the mobbed intersection and got Estelle's attention, shouting that we had to leave, and leave quickly. Estelle was unperturbed. "I'll give you four dollars," she said to one of the wall-eyed salesmen, pointing to one of the unfurled circular rugs some eight feet across. "Okay!" the man shouted, eagerly grabbing the cash from my wife's hand even as one of the other men screamed, "tree dollah!"

Estelle looked at me, smiled and said, "Would you bring these two to a taxi, please?" she pointed to two rugs lying on the potholed street. One had been purchased earlier, it seemed. Though made of straw, the big rugs were quite heavy, so I paid a couple of eager boys a dollar apiece to lug them to a taxi, where we jammed them partway into the trunk, then tying it shut.

I was obliquely aware that two militia types, in khaki uniforms and wearing U.S. Army helmet liners, had arrived. They served as police, wading into the crowd and clubbing people in the intersection with truncheons as they tried to clear the thoroughfare. Finally we got into the rattletrap taxi and slowly moved away, leaving a cloud of blue exhaust along the road to Petionville. Thus ended the great blockade of Port-au-Prince's Times Square.

After the straw rugs were safely stowed in our hotel room, I decided to see some sights with a hired car and driver while Estelle pursued further shopping possibilities in Port-au-Prince. I wanted to visit Duvalierville, named for Haiti's President for Life, Dr. Francois "Papa Doc" Duvalier. It was projected to be "The New Brasilia," a reference to the modern, concrete capital city of Brazil, which had been literally carved out of the jungle in the interior of that country only a few years earlier. *"Nous allons!"* I cried, and we were off, hurtling around, over and into crater-sized potholes in the asphalt road built by U.S. Marines during their occupation of Haiti which began in 1915.

Duvalierville turned out to be a pitiful, barely begun enterprise. Its cement buildings and triumphal arches were already crumbling, and weeds and tropical vegetation were threatening to envelop it totally. I first surmised that the great project had run out of money, but then I thought that the more likely explanation was that Papa Doc had simply decided that the money donated by the U.S. and other outside sources would be better off in his own pocket.

The only indication of enterprise I could see there was a little wooden stall whose sleeping proprietor had hung out for sale several teeshirts with Papa Doc's likeness imprinted thereon, along with the slogan, *Justice et Discipline.* This reference to justice reminded me that tourists to Haiti were assured government protection from local communist elements. Visitors were advised by Ministry of Tourism publications that they had only to point out any suspected communists to the local police, who would promptly do the disciplining necessary to result in justice.

When my guide sensed my lack of interest in Duvalierville, he took me to see some other sights, and we ended up in a village where, he said, a local witch doctor ruled supreme. Except for Papa Doc, of course. The village was incredibly poor, little more than a scattering of thatched huts around a bare open area. The witch doctor's hut was no more impressive than the others. Strangely, no one seemed to be around. I approached the hut of the witch doctor.

"No go in house of *houngan!*" shouted my driver-guide. "*Tabu!*"

I went toward the hut anyway and peeked inside. It was dark. What the hell, I thought, and went in.

Something big shot past my legs and out the door. I looked back and saw a large black dog disappearing into some bushes across the open area. Then I noticed my driver. He was standing stock-still, staring at the bushes where the black dog had gone. His mouth was open, his eyes were huge, and he was actually shaking. With the dog gone, the hut was apparently empty, and my speechless guide had no further suggestions, so I told him to return me to the hotel.

We drove back to Petionville, my driver seemingly in some state of shock. He drove the old heap of a car as fast as it would go, though the road conditions were terrible. No turning off the ignition and coasting down hills now. At the hotel I paid him, but he didn't bother to look at the money. He climbed back into the car and the tires squealed as he pulled away.

Later, I related this episode to someone who had lived in Haiti. He told me that the black dog had been the witch doctor. He had changed his outward appearance and fled the hut upon my sudden entrance. Apparently, he had not liked my vibes. That is what had spooked the driver.

Doggone, I said to myself.

Port-au-Prince: Doggedly experiencing Haiti

11

Spain:
The Cheapest and the Best

I WAS A HATCHET MAN FOR
GENERALISIMO FRANCO

I was indeed a hatchet man. Only not in the sense you might be thinking. Actually, when I was a young, sometimes university student, I worked in Spain for the Franco government, planting trees in the Sierra de Montseny, north of Barcelona. I and my fellow student-type *plantadores de árboles* were from Britain, the Continent and the U.S. (but we pointedly refrained from referring to ourselves as any sort of international brigade, as you might imagine, what with that term's connotations with the "Reds" during the not-so-distant Spanish Civil War). Before we could plant the new fir seedlings, we had to cut down the scrubby growth which then covered the mountainsides, and to do this we used bush hooks, axes – and, yes, hatchets.

But all was not work. The Spaniard running our work camp had a propensity for observing even lesser saints' days which happened to fall on a Friday or a Monday (and since virtually every day of the year is *some* saint's day, this was pretty easy to work out), so there were many long weekends during which I was able to travel around to different areas of that wonderful country, sometimes with co-workers, sometimes alone, in those halcyon days when 20 cents U.S. would buy a modest room for the night and 40 cents would buy a complete meal with wine and dessert. Bullfights, which I had discovered two years earlier in Madrid, were cheap, too. Yes, I ran with the bulls of Pamplona, without knowing what I was doing, of course.

GETTING INTERESTED IN SPAIN: A FLASHBACK

I had become fascinated with Spain when I was just a kid. All I really knew about it was from stories about Cortez, Pizzaro and the Conquistadores, and pirate movies

Spain: I was a hatchet man for Generalisimo Franco

starring Errol Flynn and Tyrone Power – even though in those films the Spanish were usually the bad guys, getting the short end of the stick in sword fights with Captain Blood and other English heroes. But I loved those morion helmets, breastplates and Toledo swords of the Spanish, and those mighty, wooden sailing ships firing broadsides.

Further, when I was twelve years old my elementary school teacher tried to infuse us with some literary culture, having us read from Washington Irving's *Tales of the Alhambra*, which enthralled me. One boy in the class was asked to read aloud from that tome, and he started out by mispronouncing the title.

"No, no!" interrupted our teacher, Miss Primm. "Boys and girls, it's not the Alham-*ber*, it's the Alham-*bra. Bra. BRA!*" Well, all this bra talk had me casting furtive glances at my precocious classmate named Lucy, who sat at a desk off to my left.

But I digress. In any case, I became most interested in Spain and I set my sights on going there – although I had to wait six more years before I could actually do it.

THE PEOPLE: HAIRY BUT NICE

In the 1950s, Spain was still struggling to recover economically from its disastrous civil war which ended in 1939. Having been friendly to Hitler (though not an actual ally) meant no Marshall Plan aid for Franco after World War II. Rather it was the tourism influx which began big time in the late 1960s – when more and more Northern Europeans began owning cars and headed for the sunny and incredibly cheap climes of Spain – that proved to be Spain's Marshall Plan. But this writing deals with the Spain of the late fifties and early sixties, before the recovery began.

The Spanish people, both young and old, were, for the most part, small (as a six-footer, I was a giant), considerably shorter than the young Spaniards of today, and they were mostly shabbily-dressed. A lot were illiterate. Many if not most women over thirty-five or forty wore black, and always would, for the rest of their lives, in mourning for a lost husband, son or other loved one(s), most likely as a result of the civil war. Even former betrothed women of dead men wore the black – some of them also for the rest of their lives. There were, of course, the exceptions: the smart señoritas and señoras of the fashionable avenues, such as the Calle Serrano of Madrid, but even these stylish ladies showed pressed-down, curled hair through their nylon stockings – no European women in the fifties, save perhaps a few fashion models and movie stars, shaved their legs or underarms. American kids used to joke about "hairy-legged European women."

A pungent, cheap-smelling tobacco smoke permeated the air of the time. It was the smell of the local cigarettes smoked by most people, which was more like the smoke of garbage cigars than cigarettes. Whenever I would smell that pungent odor in "the old days" I would know for sure I was in Spain. That smell is gone now.

Cripples were everywhere, especially men in their forties and fifties, as the French say, *mutilés de guerre*: men with one leg and a crutch, or with one arm, or multiplegic. Many served as *vigilantes*, those watchers of parking areas or keepers of the doors of locked *pensiones* at night (clap you hands in the dark, empty street, and the *vigilante* would come from out of nowhere with the key to the front door of your *pensión*), also as clerks and conductors at rail and bus stations, and other public service jobs. Getting one of these positions was probably made a lot easier if the applicant had been on Franco's side in the war.

The people were quick to be *simpático*. An example: In Madrid I stopped a businessman in a suit and tie and asked him where a certain place was. Rather than just tell me, he walked me to the sought-for location, which turned out to be several blocks away, through the narrow, twisting streets of the old part of town. I never would have found the place on my own. The man took a lot of his own time to help me, a total stranger, simply out of kindness. I of course could not offer this man money, as thanks.

Tourists were few, compared with the rest of Western Europe. Spain's reputation as a "sympathetic nation" with Nazi Germany held off a lot of tourists – possibly more Americans than Europeans. I remember that when I mentioned to some of my friends and their parents that I was planning to go to Spain, a common retort was: "Wasn't Spain on Hitler's side?" I didn't care about that; I just wanted to see Spain, which I had heard and read so much about over the years.

There were tourists in Madrid, but that was the only place I recall seeing them, in any numbers. I do remember seeing a group of American college girls on a tour there. They were all wearing shorts and had on white ankle socks, and their tanned legs were all shaved (as mentioned above, this was most un-European), and they looked like a million bucks. The Spaniards were goggle-eyed. I mean, traffic stopped. Sigh.

But there were usually very few tourists in most parts of Spain then. I saw none at all in Barcelona, and the shoulder-to-shoulder hotel megaplex of the Costa del Sol was still years away; the whole stretch from Torremolinos to Gibraltar was an empty beach, except for fishermen and their families.

There were certainly no "guest workers" – Spain was for many years the only Western European country where one could expect one's bed in a hotel room to be made by a local, and not an alien from Morocco or elsewhere.

THE HIGHWAYS AND BYWAYS OF OLD SPAIN

There were more trucks and buses than cars on the roads of Spain, all billowing out a foul-smelling exhaust from what had to have been an incredibly crude grade of diesel fuel. Even horse- and burro-drawn two-wheeled carts were everywhere.

The best roads, the national routes, were narrow, two-lane affairs, often in disrepair. And with all those big, slow trucks on them, traffic moved accordingly. A sea convoy can travel only as fast as its slowest ship; same with vehicles on a two-lane highway. Road repairs were done by men pouring tar from buckets, carried to the site by burros, a barrel strapped on each side of the animal. Many of the secondary roads were unpaved, making for slow going.

At each town limit there was a sign with the name of the *pueblo*, and as part of that sign was the Falangist Party symbol of the bunched arrows and the double yoke. Actually, this symbol was originally that of Los Reyes Católicos, Fernando and Ysabel, who were at the helm of the ship of state when the last of the muslim occupiers ("the Moors") was driven from Spain in 1492. The logo was supposed to signify productive work (the yokes) and defense of the realm (the arrows).

THE SOOTY TRAINS OF SPAIN

Spanish trains were, *sin duda*, the worst in Western Europe. They traveled on a narrower gauge track than did the trains of France, Italy, Germany, etc., and that was intentional. Railroads came to Spain late, and when they finally did so in the late 19th century, the Spanish government decided to make its rail system incompatible with that of France, in order to head off what in later years might be envisioned as a French army blitzkrieg by rail. After all, that Frenchman Bonaparte had already caused so much trouble; who knew what other terrors might come next from the north? At least a different width of track would make sure no trains loaded with French soldiers came suddenly pouring across the border at Irun or Port Bou. (Note: The Russians, wary of the Germans, did the same thing with their railroad tracks. But panzers didn't travel by rail.)

Perhaps the narrower gauge track made Spain safer from the French, but it made little difference to the passengers of RENFE (Red Nacional de Ferrocarriles Españoles – National Spanish Network of Railroads), especially the overwhelming number of them who traveled third class, as I always did. The passengers, seemingly mostly Spanish peasants going to visit relatives, always had their bags of bread, cheese, chorizo and olives, and jugs of cheap wine, and without fail they eagerly offered to share with you whatever they had. Wonderful people. On the shorter runs there were no compartments, just wooden benches back to back, down both sides of the car.

But on all train cars the only form of air conditioning was to open the window. The problem, of course, was that most locomotives pulling the trains burned coal, and the black smoke came through the open windows. But in hot or even warm weather, most people preferred a little soot to a stifling environment.

On Mallorca it was better, because the locomotives on that almond-producing island burned almond shells instead of coal, and the smoke was white. Like a Pope train. At the end of the day, your inner shirt collar wasn't black from soot, thus requiring no hand washing in your *pensión* or hotel room (or down the hall, most likely). I wonder how many people out there today remember those sooty black collar insides, from both trains and chimneys, all over Europe? Or, for the younger lot, the toilets/baths down the hall?

SPANISH CITIES: SOME STREET SCENES

There were virtually no "modern" buildings in the Spain of the 1950s. One exception was the Edificio de España (containing the Plaza Hotel), on the north side of Madrid's Plaza de España, built in the 1940s – yet even it has a Spanish flair to it, as does the 1930s-built Telefónica, on the capital's main street, now known once again as the Gran Via, but called in the Franco days la Avenida José Antonio, after the founder of the Falangist Party, José Antonio Primo de Rivera, son of an earlier dictator. In fact, the two main avenues of every Spanish city were the Avenida José Antonio and the Avenida del Generalísimo Franco.

The old buildings in the hearts of the big, industrial cities were blackish in color (like the shirt collar insides), thanks to that burning of soft coal in the winter – although Spain's city edifices were never the pitch black of those of northern Europe.

Filthier than the building façades were the public toilets of Spain. In places like railroad stations and other facilities available to the general public, things were really bad. (Oddly, the word then mostly used for toilet, *retrete*, has apparently disappeared from the modern Spanish vocabulary; the second most used word for toilets then was *aseos*, which can occasionally still be seen. But now it's usually either *servicios* or just that cartoon man-woman silhouette thing.)

You've heard the phrase, "at the edge of town." Well, most of Spain's cities really did have an edge to them. From a hilltop in the distance (for example, to the west of Sevilla), you could see the mass of the city buildings simply stop, forming an imperfect circle of jumbled buildings. Beyond the last line of houses was farmland – no more city, no suburbs, just farmland – or nothing at all. That was because nobody owned a car and therefore the end of the bus line or tram line meant the edge of the city. Simple as that. Nowadays, of course, the drab modern apartment towers go on and on for miles and miles, outside the larger cities.

Speaking of trams, those wonderful old conveyances have pretty much disappeared now, but back then they were an important equation in the mass transit formula of the cities. I remember the very large lady who jumped onto an already jam-packed streetcar rumbling along what was then Barcelona's Avenida José Antonio (now the Gran Via): she was hanging precipitously from the humanity-bulging outer platform as the tram made its way down the tree-lined avenue – some of those trees quite big and growing very close to the tram lines. She kept shouting for people to make way, to move back, as her substantial posterior was hanging out precariously toward the trees; from the packed car a man's voice rasped out, "*No hay espacio, señora – cuidado los árboles!*" ("No room, madame – be careful of the trees!") Today the old tram lanes are paved over, used as lanes for pedestrians and cyclists.

When I was a kid in the 1940s, the iceman used to come clop-clop-clopping around every day, his mule-pulled cart dripping incessantly as his big blocks of ice – meant for some people's honest-to-God iceboxes (non-electric, pre-refrigerator jobs) – slowly melted. Well, in Spain, in the old centers of the cities and in the *pueblos*, you could just as regularly hear the clanging of butcher knives, as the *cuchillero*, or knife sharpener, made his way along the street with his cart, ready to sharpen the señoras' *cuchillos* for a small sum. Home base for these knife-sharpeners in Madrid was just down the steps found in the southwest corner of the Plaza Mayor, under the big archway known as el Arco de los Cuchilleros.

In some places in southern Andalucía there was even the occasional wandering water salesman, dispensing *agua* from a big goatskin on his back, for less than one peseta per drink from a common brass cup. This was something straight out of North Africa, a Moorish practice. Two brass cups beaten together produced a clanging that meant the water man was coming.

One of the things I am starting to miss more and more as time passes are those wonderful old sleazy bars with the fabulous tapas behind the glass. A few plates of those lucullan delights, along with a caña (small beer), and I'm happy as I would be at Casa Botín. Places like this can still be found here and there – the best hunting grounds I know are the little streets near the Plaza Mayor in Madrid. But too many of these former male hangouts have become slick, modern places, with zero ambiente, loud music, and lots of female patrons. Needless to say, there were no McDonald's, KFCs, Starbucks, and so on. Nor was there a pizza joint on every corner. But lest I lapse into curmudgeondom, let us move on.

CRIME AND THE FUZZ

Petty crime was virtually nonexistant in Spain. There was a standard claim that if you dropped your wallet on a Spanish sidewalk, it would still be there the next day. Any crime which did occur was automatically blamed on gypsies.

But one most assuredly could be guilty of a Big Time Crime – and thousands were found guilty accordingly. I refer to one being – or at least arrested for being – a Red. Although the Spanish Civil War had been over for almost twenty years, the Franco government was still ever vigilant of the Red Peril. Today some scoff upon being reminded (or told) of this feature of Spanish life of that epoch, but remember that this was the time period when the USSR had launched a space satellite – and we hadn't – and Soviet Communist Party boss Khrushchev was, as I said earlier, pounding his shoe on the desk at the United Nations and bellowing to the U.S. ambassador, "We will bury you!" So a lot of people took the Red Peril threat seriously.

I found myself one time sitting in a third class train car with an English couple who lived in Spain. I had just received a letter from my father back in the U.S. and I read aloud a paragraph to the Englishman and his wife, thinking they would be interested. The news relayed by my father was that he had seen in the newspaper at home where a thousand subversives had been arrested in Andalucía by Franco's police. Well, I thought the Englishman was going to have an apoplectic fit. He "shushed" me exaggeratedly, as though we were performing in a Brian Rix farce at the Garrick Theatre in London, with the audience rolling in the aisles, laughing. But he was dead serious. He wanted me to *shut up! Now!* I replied, smiling but, admittedly, taken aback, and pointing out that, after all, we were speaking *English* in a third class Spanish train car, where the likelihood of us being understood by anyone else within earshot was surely less than nil. But my English friend was adamant. "You don't know *who* is in this car who might understand what you're saying!" he hissed in a stage whisper which, again, seemed somewhat comical to me. But I could see he was truly afraid. And, after all, he had lived here for a long time. So I shut up!

Of course, the news my father wrote to me about was never reported in the Spanish newspapers or over the radio, as there was strict censorship. I don't mention television here, because if it existed in Spain, I never saw a TV set, not even in a shop window.

There were various police entities, including traffic cops, uniformed city policemen, and those guys in trenchcoats, all trying to look like Bogey – but to me the most colorful were those men of the Guardía Civil, the traditional foot patrolmen of the highways who always traveled in pairs, with carbines slung over their shoulders. Their uniforms dated back to the nineteenth century and included enough black belts and straps to make even the most fanatical SA Brownshirt happy. But their most characteristic article of clothing was of course the black patent leather hat that most writers refer to as a tricorn, which is basically just a wide-brimmed hat turned up on three sides. The guardia's hats were turned up only on the back side. So, a dicorn, maybe?

These jolly fellows (I jest) were normally posted to an area some distance from their home provinces, the idea being that under this plan, no old friend or relative could try to get by with something while his guardia buddy winked at him. The two policemen would slowly walk along the highways and byways, occasionally flagging down a car at random, checking the occupants' papers and asking them where they were coming from, where they were going, what were their professions, why was this trip necessary, etc. I know, because I hitchhiked many a ride and more than once the car in which I was a passenger was stopped in this manner. I of course showed my passport on each occasion. After a series of questions, one of the two would hand back everyone's documents and

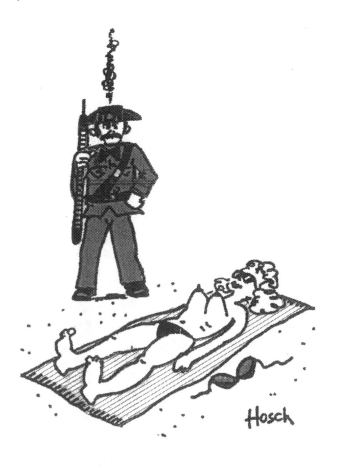

Spain: A Guardia Civil of 1958 on a beach of today

bark, *"Vayan!"*, with one hand curtly gesturing which direction we should go. Fortunately, it was always forward. But I can tell you this: if he *had* gestured straight up, we would have tried! Now, if we had been a carload of priests, we would have undergone no questioning; two snappy salutes, and we would have been on our way.

I have often mused in recent years as to what a pair of Guardia Civil minions of the old days would have done if they had, through some time warp, strolled up to one of modern-day Spain's topless beaches, because back then it was against the law for a woman to appear in public in any kind of bathing attire other than a full, one-piece swimsuit. Spain was not the Sodom and Gomorrah the French Riviera had become of late, with bikinis everywhere. Maybe one guardia would have rounded up everybody on the beach and held them at gunpoint, while his partner hiked to the nearest telephone, to call for buses or trucks to haul the offenders to jail. Or maybe they would have ordered the topless ladies to run, then shot them down, in a classic example of *la ley fuga* -- shot whilst trying to escape. Or perhaps the whole beach scene would simply have produced a mental overload for the two patrolmen, and they would have just walked on by, eyes straight ahead, seeing nothing. Like when a person, whether prankster or deranged, appears in a crowd in the nude, and the "proper people" behave as though the nude simply isn't there.

HEMINGWAY AND PAMPLONA

My interest in the Spanish matador Antonio Ordóñez had already been quite high, but it was further increased by some pages torn from a new issue of *Life* magazine and mailed to me in Spain by my father, who knew of my interest in toreo. These pages, unfolded from an envelope collected at the Barcelona office of American Express, contained the first segment of a condensed version of a new manuscript by Ernest Hemingway entitled *The Dangerous Summer*, a chronicle of the previous (1959) year's much-heralded "feud" between Ordóñez and his famous brother-in-law, Luís Miguel Dominguín, and their season-long "battle" in the plazas of España. The complete book version, the introduction to the *Life* piece said, would be published by Scribner's the following year. (I called and wrote Scribner's at least twice a year from 1961 onward, asking about the book's publication, until it finally appeared in 1985.)

Less than a month earlier, I had gotten a week off from my Spanish government-sponsored job of tree-planting in the Sierra de Montseny, to the north of Barcelona. This was possible because the youngish project director was an enthusiastic taurino whose father was a general in Franco's army and who wanted to go to the running of the bulls in Pamplona and thus simply declared the entire week a religious holiday. Only one or two others of the rather motley contingent of international student types went to the navarrese capital, the rest going elsewhere or being left to mope about the worksite with nothing to do except inevitably break into the supply of cheap, red wine stored in a monstrous clay *cántaro* in the rudimentary kitchen. All the wine would be gone when we got back, forcing abstention on everyone for several days, till more could be obtained.

After hitching rides via Barcelona and Zaragoza, by the sixth of July I was in Pamplona, and everybody there for the Fiesta de San Fermín and the annual running of the bulls through the city streets was on the lookout for Ernest Hemingway. The famous author had been there the year before, and his protégé, Antonio Ordóñez, would be appearing in the ring during this year's week-long feria. With these thoughts in mind one day, I looked across a crowded sidewalk café and saw Hemingway.

At least, I thought I saw him. It turned out that the man was another American who liked to affect a "Papa" look. Yet at the same time, the gentleman, Kenneth Vanderford, really did know a lot about the bulls. I later read, in something by Michener, that this imposing lookalike signed his name for unsuspecting autograph seekers in a manner something like the following:

"All that glitters is not gold, nor are all big men with grey beards Ernest Hemingway"

The name was hugely written, John Hancock style. Then Mr. Vanderford would sign his own name, very small, down below.

The autograph hounds would thank the man profusely, walking off in a sort of daze as they admired what they were convinced was the bona fide signature of Ernest Hemingway.

I was in Pamplona for the bulls, but also for the non-stop fiesta I'd learned about from Hemingway's celebrated book, *The Sun Also Rises.* I had met some other young Americans along the way, and together we had found a place to stay in a Spanish family's old, pitch-dark flat, on one of Pamplona's tiny side streets. We paid about a dollar a day apiece for half of a double bed each, which seemed like highway robbery to us at the time, but we realized we were fortunate to find anything at all, at any price.

Determined to comport myself in a manner which would have made Hemingway proud of me, I set out on the first afternoon to celebrate the Fiesta de San Fermín, or simply *los sanfermines*, as the cognoscenti refer to it, with the proper macho demeanour. I didn't have any white pants to wear, following tradition, as did most of the other *mozos* (young men) in the streets, but I did at least have on the long-sleeved white shirt which was the other half of the uniform, to wear with my khakis. And around my neck I tied a red bandanna, which was virtually compulsory.

As the afternoon turned into evening, my coterie of companions waxed and waned. Finally, however, after many hours of frantic camaraderie and countless liters of vino corriente tinto, the last of my new friends had given up and gone to bed, or to sleep, in any case, so it was alone that I walked out into Pamplona's Plaza del Castillo, still the centre of vibrant animation, even in the hour before dawn. I walked past one young man, asleep on a sidewalk as dawn approached. He had sported a nice, long ponytail – which someone had neatly cut off and left lying next to him, including the rubber band holding the base of it in place.

A band of young musicians, clad in their already dirty white outfits and red bandannas, created quite a bit of enthusiastic noise with their instruments, while others danced around them, snapping their fingers. They looked livelier than ever.

I was caught up in watching a group of Spanish boys, most of them in their twenties. They were weaving down the street, five or six abreast, each with his arms around the neck of the person on either side of him. I found myself on one end of the line, being dragged down a winding street, while the others sang some spirited Spanish song I was not familiar with. As we rolled on down the street, sending people scuttling out of our way, we each improvised little dance steps of our own. It was sort of like a chorus line on a night when a prize was to be awarded for the most individualistic participant.

After many choruses and many blocks, I was worn out. The others must have been equally exhausted, because when someone suggested we sit down for a minute to take a breather, we all flopped down on the curb without a word. By now the night was gone and everything was a bright grey, but the eternal partying continued unabated all around us.

We were in a widened street, and there was an unusually large crowd, all men, milling about, and I noticed in passing that this bunch seemed a little more sober-acting than usual. Then an aerial bomb exploded, and the people all cheered. I sat there, still panting. They've started with the fireworks again, I thought to myself. But there was a noticeable change in the crowd. An air of excitement was building, but I wasn't sure why.

A little bell was beginning to ring in the back of my rioja-washed mind, but it was drowned out by the 'boom' of another aerial bomb. The whole world seemed to erupt in screams, and everyone around me began running like crazy up the street. Everything was suddenly crystal clear. I had stumbled across the Calle Santo Domingo, smack in the middle of the world-famed *encierro*, and the huge, black fighting bulls, which would appear in the plaza de toros that afternoon, were at that very moment pounding up the street directly at me.

I was already on my feet and running before I ever finished this train of thought. There wasn't any time for thinking, only running. And running was the only answer, for all the doorways on both sides of the narrow street were either shut tight, or, if recessed, packed with onlookers. I cast a quick glance over one shoulder as I charged up the street, stumbling on the cobblestones and bumping into other runners. I could see the first two of the bulls about ten yards behind me, and believe me, they weren't loafing. Now, it is a supposed fact that a man cannot outrun a bull.

But I can assure you, I was doing my best to prove that theory fallacious.

There was a small group of men between me and the bulls, but most of the crowd was far ahead. The side streets were fenced off with heavy wooden railings to keep the runners and the bulls all on track up the Calle Estafeta and to the bullring. Anybody who had thoughts about abandoning the foot race and exiting through one of these fenced-off areas could think again. First of all, the wooden barricades were packed solid with onlookers, and tradition demanded that these people not permit any suddenly chickenhearted soul to get out of the path of the charging bulls, meaning that anyone trying to do so would find himself being pushed back into the street by the mob on the other side of the barrier. And if that wasn't enough, a policeman was stationed at each such intersection, and if necessary he would use his long wooden truncheon to pummel would-be escapers back into the Calle Estafeta with a certain grim satisfaction. Thus men were leaping from the street onto the walls of buildings, grabbing signs, grillworks and anything else they could use to hoist themselves up from the street. Others dived to the edge and lay huddled next to the buildings, their hands clasped over they heads. Still other fell sprawling in the street. I was one of this lot.

It all happened so quickly that it was over before I could start thinking. As soon as I hit the pavement, someone tripped over me. Three or four other men jumped over me, a couple of them using me as a stepping stone. Then, before I could move, the bulls were upon me. Fortunately, I was off to one side of the street and only one of the bulls stepped on me. Actually, he scraped the side of my right leg with a hoof, but it still hurt, and it was close enough to being stepped on to suit me. When the bulls had passed on by, the crowd which runs after them thundered over me, adding a couple more bruises for good measure.

I got up and resumed running, wiping bloodied hands on my filthy white shirt. I was aware of a woman watching from a grilled window. She gasped, covering her mouth with one hand and pointing at me with the other. I must have looked pretty bad, because my ripped pants were also bloody in several places, as a result of my fall and the inconsiderate bull.

The crowd was disappearing up the street now. Some boys jumped into the *calle* from the barricades at intersections and raced after the others, intent on seeing the climax of the encierro from inside the plaza de toros. I'd gone through this much of it, so I figured I might as well see the rest. Breathing raggedly, I jogged up the street as fast as I could.

At the end of the street, where it emptied into the broad area in front of the bullring, more wooden fences funneled both the two-legged and four-legged runners in through a wide doorway on one side of the circular building. I stumbled through the big door just as two attendants were preparing to close it. I knew that the full-grown fighting bulls which had just run through the streets would be removed from the crowded circle of the bullring as soon as possible, but that before this act could be carried out, a few young men would most likely get tossed around, if not gored. Then smaller cows of the same fighting bull stock but with padded horns, which could easily break a few bones, nevertheless, would be ushered in, one or two at a time, with a couple of hundred or more would-be *novilleros* awaiting them. The seats of the bullring were filled with people watching the event from a safer vantage point.

After the fighting bulls had raised havoc for a couple of minutes, during which time one man was severely battered by one of the 1300-pound animals, the attendants, with the help of steers, cleared the ring of the bulls, and the fans sat back and waited for the next act.

In a few minutes, a roar went up from the crowd, as the first padded-horned *vaquilla* (fighting cow) burst into the arena, catching one man off guard and tossing him about five feet in the air. Its eyes wide open and its nostrils flaring, the lean black animal charged into the crowd. In its blind fury, it had selected no single target, and everyone managed to stay clear of it. It stopped in the centre of the ring, breathing hard, then charged in my direction. Once again the would-be macho types, including me, eluded the covered horns. After two or three more unsuccessful forays, the cow wised up. It charged again, heading for a man in a blue shirt. The man changed his direction, as everyone had been doing, but this time the *vaquilla* ignored the shouts and taunts of others and turned with the man. All of the man's efforts to escape proved fruitless, and at last a great roar of approval came from the crowd as the man sailed into the air, tossed by the horns of the victorious *vaca*.

After a few minutes, the first cow was taken out of the arena, and everyone waited for the second. About twenty young men, either very bold or very stupid, seated themselves, jammed together, on the sand immediately in front of the gateway through which the next *vaquilla* would enter. When it did, it leaped over the majority of the boys, but managed to knock over three or four of them with its back legs, just as a horse sometimes knocks the top rung off a hurdle during a steeplechase. The crowd cheered.

This *vaquilla* took a different approach from the last. It immediately headed for the barrera, the wooden fence over which many of the aspiring toreros jumped when things got too close for comfort, and began a circuit of the arena, with one of its padded horns only an inch or two from the red boards. To the delight of the onlookers in the seats, many a would-be fence-jumper was hooked and brusquely dumped over the barrera and into the *callejón* as he attempted to scale the wooden wall to safety.

Before the sixth and last fighting cow of the morning was led out of the ring, I managed to try out a couple of passes, using the sweater I had worn during the night, later tying it around my waist with its sleeves. I didn't get tossed, but that's about all I can say for my performance. I also didn't get beaten up by some of the Spaniards, as did a young man from Texas who jumped on the back of one cow and tried to ride it, rodeo style.

At last it was all over, and the people began filing out of the plaza de toros, and ready to renew the revelry interrupted by the encierro, but others, including myself, bent on sleeping for a while.

I and my friends went to the daily bullfight that afternoon and every day thereafter, joining what without a doubt were, and still are, the noisiest, wildest and most undisciplined crowds to witness *la Fiesta Nacional* anywhere in Spain. Six different bands of *peñas*, or bullfight clubs, were in the cheaper, sunny side seats, all playing various *paso dobles* and the local *riau-riau* music of Navarra, in direct competition with each other, while the shouting aficionados in their wine-stained white clothes quaffed vino from leather wineskin *botas* and sloppily ate huge, long loaf sandwiches they'd brought with them. The coat and tie wearing purists of Sevilla and Madrid, who are quick to quiet anyone even speaking during serious moments at a *corrida*, would have been horrified.

On the second morning, I watched the running of the bulls from the balcony of an old house facing the Calle

Estafeta, paying a few pesetas for the privilege. I was both awed and sobered by the dramatic turmoil passing beneath me, and I breathed a sigh of relief as I decided that my encierro days belonged to yesterday, when I was young and foolish.

All too soon, La Fiesta de San Fermin was over, and I and the others returned to the Sierra de Montseny and our tree-planting.

(Hemingway never showed, and a year later he was dead.)

A PLANTADOR DE ARBOLES

My job, as mentioned, was planting trees in the Sierra de Montseny, about seventy kilometers north of Barcelona. Our work camp was quite primitive, two stone buildings with dirt floors serving as dormitory and kitchen/community room on a mountainside overlooking a broad valley far below. At night the glow from the lights of Barcelona could be seen in the sky to the southwest. Water was from a mountain spring a hundred meters or so along the mountain, while the toilet was a plank across a fork in a tree branch jutting out over the edge of a cliff, in the other direction from the spring.

Work days began with our motley group of students from various European countries and the U.S. gathering in a ragged formation in a flat area to the side of the stone buildings, facing a crooked flagpole cut from a small tree and from which flew the red and yellow flag of Spain. At this daily assembly, one of the duties of our work camp director, the thirtyish Spaniard called José, was to lead us in singing the Falangist Party hymn, *Cara al Sol:*

> *Cara al sol con la camisa nueva,*
> *Que tu bordaste en rojo ayer . . .*

At first I and most of the other non-Spanish students objected to this insertion of Spanish politics into our daily lives, but we soon adapted and "rolled with the punch". You see, our leader, José, was a devoted, blue-shirted *falangista* whose father was a general in Franco's army, and he had the power to permit or deny independent weekend travel away from the camp. Since I was keen to hitchhike into Barcelona to attend the weekly Sunday *corridas*, and as others wanted to go elsewhere over the weekend as well, we soon learned to humor José by singing the Falangist anthem each morning, at first reluctantly, and then increasingly with a mock-gusto "I can sing it louder than you can" ebullience. And we weren't pressed to do the straight-armed salute, although the Spanish guys did it. Pleased, José granted us verbal exit visae each Friday afternoon after work, and off we would go, most to the beach at Arenys (at least during the summer months), but me Barcelona bound.

The work camp was Spartan but I enjoyed it immensely. I liked the international student makeup of the work force, young men from Sweden, Denmark, Germany, Britain, Spain, the United States, and some other countries which I can't remember, plus three French girls who did the cooking. The altitude, 1500 meters/4800 feet or so, was high enough to keep the temperature fairly moderate in summer, although later on it would become downright cold and snow would sometimes fall.

On one occasion I and three colleagues outsmarted ourselves. Three of my tree-planting co-workers and I were returning to our mountain work camp one evening following a roundtrip walk of six miles or so to the nearest civilization, a gloomy, stone-built mountain hotel with never any guests in evidence, where we bought *gaseosa* and some rather basic hard candy. As we left the one-lane asphalt mountain road and started up a trail though the woods to our dirt-floored mountainside stone hut *sin agua o electricidad*, we paused and admired a big cherry tree alongside a solitary Spanish woodsman's house. We could see hundreds, maybe thousands, of big, luscious, bright red cherries, all just begging to be picked and scoffed down. Up the tree we went.

What a feast we had! And considering that out diet at the work camp consisted almost exclusively of bread, onions, tomatoes, olive oil and a few bits of gristly lamb from time to time (but plenty of cheap red wine which we all chipped in and bought by the huge *cántaro*, at ten cents U.S. per liter), those fat, juicy cherries seemed something really special. We were up in the tree, laughing, eating and talking with our mouths full and cherry juice running down our chins when we heard the voice.

"Ajá! Ladrones, eh?" Robbers!

We looked down at the base of the tree and saw a stocky, middle-aged man wearing a flannel shirt, corduroy pants, boots and beret – and with a shotgun in his grasp. We of course immediately ceased our epicurean pursuits and stared warily at him. He told us in no uncertain terms to get our posteriors out of that tree, *pronto* – and we hastily obliged. When we were all on the ground the man approached us menacingly and said only: "Start running!" He began shifting the shotgun to his shoulder. Needing no prompting, the four of us lit out, running like hell for the forest, fifty yards away.

That was the longest fifty yards I ever ran. My old high school football coach would have been amazed at my newfound speed, I am sure, but even so, it seemed to take forever. And I swear I could hear that shotgun's twin hammers being cocked, even as I ran. Which of us would he shoot first?

Spain: "Start Running!"

Or could he hit us all with two shots from a distance? Depends on whether he was loaded for birds or for bear, I thought, my legs and heart pumping wildly.

Then we were in the woods. Each of us instinctively selected his own large tree to cower behind, as cover, while we caught our breath. Fifty yards away the old woodsman was laughing his head off.

We threw up the cherries and trudged back to the camp.

A GERMAN DINGBAT IN SPAIN

I was dogged at this time by a German youth who worked with me. Wolfgang was the fellow's name, a North German as I recall, from somewhere near Hamburg. He was not exactly an Aryan poster boy, being rather short and with a big mop of wild brown hair above an intelligent, sharp-featured face dominated by a big pair of hornrimmed glasses. He was a smart kid with an excellent command of English (though, ironically, not Spanish), the result of a British tutor, he said, but he could get on your nerves. Why he chose to follow me around I couldn't figure – I would have preferred he'd followed after someone else, someplace else, but I found him tagging along behind me in Barcelona one weekend. I hadn't traveled the seventy kilometers or so from the work camp with him. Rather, he just turned up at my elbow as I was buying a cheap *sol* ticket at the Plaza de Toros Monumental. Wolfgang was weird. He shadowed me, yet he tormented me.

"You Americans!" he snorted. "You are disgusting! You like the bullfights because you are not a serious people. You enjoy a medieval spectacle of torture and the things of the Marquis de Sade because you have no culture of your own. Why do you not enjoy instead some things of true culture?"

"Like maybe a torchlight parade with a book roast at the end?" I asked.

"Excuse me?" said Wolfgang, nonplussed.

"Skip it," I said. "Anyway, most Americans *don't* like bullfights. I'm one of the exceptions. Hey, are you going in?"

"Pah!" snorted Wolfgang, walking off. But he did buy a ticket, because I saw him later, sitting a couple of sections away in the top row of the roofed-over *andanada sol*, his back against the wall.

[I realize this dialog from so long ago might be suspect, but despite the intervening years most of these conversations are as clear in my mind as though they took place yesterday. I stand by all these quotes, some in essence but others practically *ver batim*.]

After the corrida I went across the street to a popular bar, jammed on this day with American sailors, and, standing at the bar, I invested ten pesetas, or sixteen cents U.S., in a bottle of San Miguel cerveza. At a table on the sidewalk it would've cost me twelve pesetas. I was no dummy.

Suddenly, there was Wolfgang. He wasn't drinking anything, because he wasn't a fatcat American spendthrift like me. He was just hovering there at my side.

"Did you enjoy the *corrida*, Wolfgang?" I asked him.

"Pah! I go because a person must see even the bad things. If I do not see it myself, I cannot be sure it is truly so bad as I think maybe it is. So I go!"

"So you liked it, huh?"

The reaction was instantaneous. "Pah! *Nein!* No! Germans do not like the bullfights," he pronounced. "It is too cruel. It is a barbarian thing. How can an American like this thing? Or an Englishman? The Spanish, ah, that I can understand, because the Spanish, they are, you know, *Untermenschen*. And the French, they are even worse. Pah!

But the Americans and the English, you are almost like us, you know? Not quite, but almost. But not *Untermenschen*. You know *Untermensch?*"

"Yeah, Wolfgang," I sighed. "I know *Untermensch*. At least what you mean by *Untermenschen*. Subhumans. As opposed to you and yours, right?" Wolfgang shrugged but said nothing, so I went on: "You say Germans don't like the bullfight because it's too cruel. Don't you think maybe killing six million people in death camps is – just maybe – a little more cruel than liking bullfights?"

Wolfgang's face turned purple and he exploded. "Lies! All those stories are lies! Lies fabricated by the enemies of Germany! It is not enough that Germany was beaten to her knees! Even now the German people must be made into monsters so that the world will not respect us! All done with lies! Lies!"

Thus spake not Zarathustra, I mused, but Josef Goebbels. And this fellow had only been a little kid when the bad doktor und Der Führer und zeir Loved Ones had chomped down onto their L-pills and/or blown their brains out in der Bunker. I sighed again.

"Wolfgang, you're a dingbat."

"What is this dingbat? I do not know this word." He looked at me suspiciously.

I hesitated, then lied, "Oh, it just means something like, er, an intelligent but very difficult person."

Wolfgang pursed his lips and thought about this, then spoke. "Yes," he said. "Yes, then I am for sure a dingbat!"

TO THE SOUTH OF SPAIN

One weekend I had, as usual, attended the Sunday *corrida* at Barcelona's Plaza Monumental, as well as a nighttime *novillada* (*un nocturno*) with *novilleros* (apprentice bullfighters) at the other bullring, the Plaza Arenas.

Afterward, I returned to a little bar a block away, where the bartender had agreed to hold my traveling gear for me during the *novillada*. This weekend – fortunately, as it turned out – I had brought my small fabric suitcase and all my possessions with me from the tree-planting camp to Barcelona. Often I carried much less, although even at such times I would still be carrying hygienic equipment as well as my own bed -- my belongings consisting of a toothbrush rolled up inside a Spanish Army blanket tied with a piece of frazzled cord. There were some comfortable benches in a little park along the Calle Layetana, and if one arrived early enough in the evening to claim a free one, it was yours for the night. The click-click-click of manual hedgeclippers outside an adjacent ministry building of some sort at seven the next morning generally served as a stand-in alarm clock. And the Spanish soldier in the German coal-scuttle helmet with his carbine at the ready would have provided security, I suppose, had such been necessary – although nothing could have been more superfluous, in reality. Street crime simply didn't exist in Spain, in that day and time. Anybody stupid enough to try it and who got caught could pretty well count on being stood up against a wall. A good deterrent.

Anyway, in the bar near the Plaza Arenas the bartender was talking to some patrons about upcoming *corridas* and *ferias* in Barcelona and elsewhere. This was of interest to me, as such information was hard to come by. The man was saying that he'd heard Antonio Ordóñez would be back at the Malaga *feria* just now getting under way, and the news got my attention, especially as I did not know at the time that the bartender was full of it.

I decided to take a few days off from work, without pay of course, and go to Malaga, despite the distance and the effort. Sure, I could probably hitchhike my way there – eventually. But the road traffic in Spain was only a fraction of what it was in, say, France, and the majority of the transit consisted of big, lumbering trucks and vans spewing foul-smelling black clouds of diesel fumes and usually traveling at top speeds of 30 mph or less. And driving though the narrow, winding streets of even a medium-sized city en route could require half an hour at less than walking speed. I hadn't had much luck getting lifts from the drivers of these commercial vehicles, anyway, and most of the drivers of the few private cars – the Spaniards, at least – were of a social class which generally precluded their even considering stopping for a hitchhiker.

There was a curve on the southwestern edge of Barcelona which was favored by ride-seekers, as traffic had to slow for the bend in the road and there was a wide dirt area under some big, shady eucalyptus trees where one could easily pull off and stop. Once I got a ride there with four drunk sergeants of the U.S. Air Force in a yellow '57 Ford convertible, who drove me down the coast to the beach at Sitges. Another time I rode in the back of a pickup truck for maybe fifty kilometers, my travel companion a huge pig tethered to a ring in the truck's floor, but I could've *walked* as fast as that old junker went. No, I told myself, for Malaga I would have to go by train. Unfortunately, although it was by no means expensive, it was a very long way to go – about the same distance as from my home in Atlanta to the Canadian border at Windsor, and via the most antiquated highway and/or rail systems to be found in Western Europe.

I was told that the problem with going to Malaga by train was that, day after day, the sign in the Barcelona railroad station said *completo* over the *taquilla* for trains to Valencia and points south, which included Malaga. I went to the station and saw the "sold out" sign. I moped around the big, gloomy and grimy rail terminal for a while, buying some cheap food and taking advantage of the public toilet facilities, always in short supply in Spain. Now, being realistic about it, just about *everything* public was dirty and neglected, the result of a crippling lack of funds available, but *nothing* rivaled the condition of *los aseos* in the train stations. Finally, despite the *completo* sign, I just boarded a train anyway, *sin billete*, something technically unlawful. A kindly old one-armed conductor, one of a vast army of paraplegics then seen everywhere in Spain, relics of the Civil War, allowed me to buy a ticket from him as far as Tarragona, fifty miles or so down the track. He told me to stand in the vestibule at the end of the car and to buy a proper ticket in Tarragona; so far, so good. At Tarragona I jumped off the train and ran into the terminal – along with several Spaniards who were doing the same thing I was – and, although Valencia tickets were sold out, I was able to buy one to Tortosa, another fifty miles further on. And so it went, all the way to Valencia.

The train finally pulled into Valencia's main station located adjacent to the plaza de toros at nine o'clock that evening, almost ten hours after leaving Barcelona, 200 miles to the northeast. All of the time had been spent standing or, at best, leaning on a wall or against a railing. The train had been packed, and I was by no means the only traveler without a seat.

An American about my age had also boarded the train at Barcelona, and we stood and chatted for hours. He had been financing his travels in Spain over the past year or more by working as an extra in various Hollywood epic movies being filmed there because the scenery and weather were great and costs were but a tiny fraction of what they would have been at home.

"I was in *John Paul Jones* last year," the kid told me. "I have one really great scene where I'm dressed up like a ship's officer and I'm standing next to Robert Stack while he unrolls a map in the captain's cabin of the ship, which was really just a set. I don't say anything, but I look back and forth from Robert Stack to this other fellow, while they talk. Go see the movie – you'll see me" [I did, some months later. Damned if the guy wasn't there, just like he said.]

"This year I've been working on *King of Kings*," the fellow went on. "My best part in that one is when I and a bunch of other guys are shaking our fists at Jeffrey Hunter – he's Jesus, you know – and yelling, 'Crucify him!' In the first take, we threw paper-mâché rocks at him, but the Spanish extras got all upset about that and threatened to walk off, so they did away with the 'rocks' on the other takes."

I asked how Hunter handled the role of Christ. "Oh, he was okay," my new friend replied, "at least at first. But, you know, I really think the part went to his head. After a while he got to where he wouldn't speak to anybody, just slowly walked around in his robe and beard, like he was in a holy daze or something, know what I mean? But you know what was even weirder than that? When we were shooting crowd scenes and he'd come walking up to a bunch of those Spanish extras, they'd all fall to their knees and start crossing themselves like he was the real thing! The director's people got so pissed off! Here these Spaniards are all supposed to be yelling for Jesus's head, and instead they're on their knees crossing themselves! It was wild!"

My film star friend paused, then shook his head wistfully. "I wish I could've been in that movie they made here the year before I got here, the one about the huge cannon in Napoleonic times, and starring Cary Grant and Sophia Loren."

"Oh, yeah," I said. "I saw that one. *The Pride and the Pizza*."

"*The Pride and the Passion*," the budding thespian corrected me. "Yeah, that would've been great. That Loren broad's got some knockers on her."

Valencia had recently wound up its yearly July *feria*, and strings of lights still hung from lampposts and trees in the Plaza del Caudillo, the main square of the city. Otherwise, the place was dirty and dead as a doornail. For my dinner, I bought a "strawberry milkshake" at the Bar San Remo, opposite the bullring. It was horrible. It didn't taste like strawberries and I don't think there was any milk – much less ice cream – in it. At least it was cheap.

MALAGA

After a night in one of those cheap little *pensiones* to be found in the street alongside the Valencia rail station, I resumed my journey by train southward to Malaga, traveling through the vast orange groves of the Huerta de Valencia, with the blue Mediterranean off to the east.

At long, long last I stood out front of the Malaga rail terminal, my ratty little suitcase in my hand; this was before backpacks had become *de rigueur* for young cheapo American travelers. The August night was warm and sultry as I walked east, crossing the Rio Guadalmedina and heading into the old part of town. I just asked the way to la Avenida José Antonio, since the main street of just about every city in Franco's Spain was named for the martyred Falangist Party founder, the son of dictator Primo de Rivera, of the 1920s. José Antonio was an attractive boulevard lined by big plane trees and palms and running parallel to the harbor – in fact, continuing straight on to the pretty Plaza de Toros La Malagueta, at the end. I found a room in the same peeling-stucco apartment building *pensión* where I'd stayed two years earlier, a place with French windows facing onto the wide avenue, not far from Malaga's finest hotel, the venerable old Miramar, whose bar was the gathering spot for local *taurinos*.

The broad, shaded thoroughfare was the site of Malaga's yearly *feria* – at least the carnival-like portion of the event. Years later it would be moved to a dusty hillside on the edge of town, but at this time the big trees downtown sheltered stalls selling food and drink, tents housing simple games of chance with a stuffed animal as the grand prize, and motorized sling-'em / whip-'em rides such as *El Azote* and *El Pulpo*. There was even a small ferris wheel opposite the ornate post office building. In the very center of the city, where Calle Larios joined José Antonio, locals in traditional Andalusian finery rode handsome steeds or reclined in horsedrawn carriages for equine promenades.

The *feria* had already been underway for three days, but I could still see six *corridas* if I stayed till the end. The prices weren't too bad: I could get a seat in the *andanada sol* for forty cents U.S. After my first *corrida* of the *feria* I was wandering around in the old part of town and found a particularly cheap sidewalk café. I sat down and ordered my daily bottle of cerveza, then pulled something to read out of my back pocket. There was still plenty of light for reading, even at 9:00 p.m., at this time of the year.

I had a copy of *Europe on $5 a Day*, a dogeared paperback someone had left behind in the horrible youth hostel in Barcelona and which I had subsequently nationalized for the common good: mine. The book was full of tips for budding budget travelers, and it trumpeted the claim that five dollars, managed judiciously, could cover the daily cost of one's accommodations (share double basis) and three frugal meals daily, but the amount excluded transportation, entertainment and miscellaneous. Me, I was averaging *half* that, *single* basis, *including* the transportation, miscellaneous, et al., on the days when I was on the road.

Suddenly someone plopped down in the chair opposite mine at the small table.

Wolfgang.

He said nothing, he just glared at me.

"Wolfgang," I said. Jesus, I thought.

"Yes, it is I," he said, dead serious. "I did not know you were in Malaga. I have come to the South to see more of Spain."

"As I recall, I mentioned to you that I was thinking about coming here for the *feria*," I ventured.

"No, you said nothing to me. I just come to the South of Spain."

"But you won't be going to the corridas, because you don't like them."

"That is correct. It is an ugly and cruel spectacle."

"Good," I mumbled.

Wolfgang's eyebrows shot up. "It is *good* that such a cruel and bad thing exists, and that you go to it?"

"Uh, no, no," I said. "That's not what I meant." I closed my book and laid it on the table. Wolfgang stared at it, reading the title upside down.

"Look at this!" he cried, pointing at said book. "Who but Americans would spend so much money traveling in Europe? It is so crazy, spending all that money! Do you know that Americans use and waste more of everything – fuel, electricity, food, everything – than all the rest of the world put together?"

"I don't really think so, Wolfgang," I said.

"Yes! Yes! It is true!"

"Even if it were," I replied, "so what?"

"So, it is not right! Why should America have all these things?"

"Why not? If Germany had won the war, don't you think your country would be in the same position?"

"Yes, of course. But that would be different, because then we would be the victors!"

"*Natürlich*," I said, rolling my eyes. "How stupid of me not to have realized that."

"Yes." Said Wolfgang.

One day after a *corrida* a La Malagueta, with Wolfgang nowhere to be seen, I poked my head into the bar at the Miramar. I wasn't even considering buying a drink there – it was the most expensive place in town – but I liked rubbing elbows with the taurine crowd, even if only for a few minutes. The patrons, Spanish gentlemen, wore coats and ties and so did I, my only coat and my only tie, both somewhat the worse for wear. I noticed a stout, balding, middle-aged fellow who looked British – navy blue blazer, white shirt with red silk cravat, gray flannel slacks and red face – who was surreptitiously draining the remains of leftover drinks around the room. He didn't seem to be with anyone, so I struck up a conversation with him. His name was Cyril or Nigel or some such, and he was from England. Originally. Now he lived in Malaga. Reading between the lines, I eventually gathered that he was the black sheep of some respectable family back in Fair Albion who was being paid a small but regular stipend to stay in Spain and away from England. He's got an impressive accent and air about him,

I thought – for a bum. He also had a good sense of humor and an interest in *los toros*, so he was fun to talk to. And interesting. He told me about Ronda, in the mountains not too far away, and I became determined to go there. Lord Blacksheep offered to guide me there in my car, if I might see my way clear to "pick up lunch and a libation or two" for the two of us, in return for a "first class tour guide job." When I told him I had virtually no money, much less a car, he mumbled, "Oh, dear!" and wandered off. But the seed was planted. Now I must see Ronda!

After the *feria* was over I checked and discovered that there were no trains to Ronda. In fact, Malaga was the end of the rail line of the south. There were no towns of any size along the Mediterranean down the coastline to Gibraltar, seventy-five miles away, just nearby Torremolinos and then a few fishing villages and long stretches of empty beaches. Public transportation to Ronda, it seemed, would have to be by bus.

ON TO RONDA

The greatest virtually overnight change in physical appearance to any of the world's geographical areas was surely that which Spain's Costa del Sol experienced in the mid-1960s. Incidentally, the name "Costa del Sol" was brand new when I first made a trip by bus down that underpopulated strip of coastline. This romantic appellation, like those of Spain's other "Costas," was an idea of the country's Ministry of Tourism at that time, an effort to increase tourism to the country's beautiful but empty coasts which were not being exploited by rich foreigners.

By the late sixties, many Northern Europeans finally were beginning to have money, leisure time and personal automobiles for the first time, and the borders with France at Irún and Port Bou suddenly experienced a flood of sun-starved English, German and Scandinavian tourists bound for a pleasant land where their money went much further than it did at home, and where the sun actually shined.

But at the beginning of that same decade, things remained virtually unchanged from centuries past. Marbella was still a sleepy little whitewashed village with red tile roofs, narrow, winding, cobblestone streets, no resort hotels, and no tourists. The town's houses along the beach faced not the Mediterranean, but inland onto the thin, potholed coastal road running from Malaga to Algeciras. On the beach itself, as elsewhere along this stretch, there were no foreigners sunning themselves – just small fishing boats painted green and blue and white, canted over to one side, with a few fishermen wearing faded blue work clothing and caps, mending nets on the sand.

The only exception to all this was the little town of Torremolinos, just beyond Malaga's combination military/civilian airport on the south side of the city. Here there was a handful of small tourist hotels and *pensiones* gathered around a tiny central plaza through which ran the coast road. There were no hotels on the beach, which was a walk of a quarter mile down the hillside, but it was close enough to be usable by European visitors, if not American. For the latter, there was one hotel just to the south of Torremolinos which was close enough to the beach to be acceptable. This was the new Hotel Pez Espada, the very first of what would eventually be thousands of modern hostelries, big and small, built for international vacationers along this length of coastline. Indeed, even by 1968 the entire character of this edge of Spain had changed beyond recognition. But, as

I say, a few years earlier, the boom had not yet begun and everything was still more or less as it had always been.

The bus I boarded at the *Estación de Autobuses de Málaga* was of the U.S. school bus variety, except smaller. Another difference was that each aisle seat on the righthand side had a single fold-up seat affixed to it by hinges and a spring. These extra seats could be pushed down and fastened into place against the other aisle seat, meaning that a row now had five seats across instead of four. It also, of course, meant that there was no longer any aisle, as the folded-down seat took up that space. As it turned out, all of the bus's seats were occupied, including these aisle seats. Thus when the ticket collector, a one-legged old fellow with a crutch, began torturously working his way toward the rear of the bus, it was necessary for each person occupying a fold-down seat to stand, fold up his or her seat and let the ticket collector squeeze past, then reverse the process. Obviously, once the man had made it all the way to the back of the bus, the awkward act had to be repeated in the other direction. All the while, the bus bounced and careened violently.

For the first few kilometers, I confess, I felt guilty, for I had slinked my way to the bus station like a thief in the night, in an effort to avoid being spotted by a Wolfgang whom I suspected was out there somewhere. Eventually, however, I forgot about him. Meanwhile, the conveyance trundled on down the coast road built in 1928 during the reign of King Alfonso XIII and apparently not repaired since. As everywhere in Spain, at the edge of each town or village, alongside the highway with the city limit sign, there was the large, burgundy-colored, yoked arrow symbol of the Partida Falange. This symbol was also often seen paint-stenciled on the walls of buildings, particularly government ones. Sometimes the stenciled silhouette of the Generalísimo accompanied it.

From time to time we would pass a crumbling old stone watchtower built by the Moors to keep a lookout for enemy vessels, in the times before the final liberation of Andalucía – the muslims' last stronghold in Spain – by Christian forces of Los Reyes Católicos in 1492. We also passed a superannuated *cuartel* of the Guardia Civil, an ochre-colored, two-story stucco barracks built on a curve overlooking the sea. A few of the guardias' wives were hanging laundry on a clothesline in the bright sunlight, and some small children played in the dirt nearby.

On a hilltop I saw my favorite billboard to be found along the highways of Spain: the big, black silhouette of a *toro bravo*. In large white letters on the bull the word *Osborne* identified the sponsoring company, and in smaller, yellow letters below, the word *Veterano* touted a specific brandy produced by the big firm making nice things out of grapes.

Eventually we arrived in the tiny crossroads hamlet of San Pedro de Alcántara, where the road to Ronda wound from the coast up into the mountains. Here I left the bus, thanking the lady who had sat in front of me for her hospitality. At a brief stop at the little one-story house which served as the municipal bus station in Marbella, local women selling homemade baked goods had pitched their wares to the passengers through the bus's open windows. The aforementioned lady in front of me had purchased some white delicacies, offering me one. I accepted, with thanks. The thing turned out to be some sort of unsweetened blob of meringue which was hard as a rock and totally tasteless. As soon as I could discreetly do so, I had dropped it out the window.

My first bus chugged away toward Algeciras, and in a little while the one to Ronda left with me and several passengers from the last bus, plus a few new ones from San Pedro. It had the same fold-down aisle seats, but, thankfully, it was not full and the aisle remained clear. The vehicle's engine strained increasingly as the grade became steeper, the driver constantly downshifting. Particularly as Ronda was a well-known place, I was surprised at how poor the road was. After we got into the mountains themselves, the bumpy asphalt highway narrowed to a single lane which wound its way precariously around and up cliffsides. Every so often there would be a widened spot off to the side away from the precipitous dropoff, and here the driver of any vehicle traveling in the opposite direction who could see the bus coming could pull off and allow us to continue on. More than once, despite much horn-blowing in advance, we came suddenly face to face with an oncoming car or truck, always on a sharp curve around an outcrop of cliff. Brakes would slam on, then the vehicle nearest to a pull-off place would have to very carefully back up along the guardrail-less cliffside niche of road, one time as far as a quarter mile or more. Some of the bus's passengers, I noted, refused to look out the windows on the cliff side. In many places the drop was probably a thousand feet or more, almost straight down.

In just a few years the bottoms of those ravines as well as others all over Spain would be littered with the rusting hulks of automobiles. Here is what happened: Spaniards who heretofore had not been able to afford a car, finally – with the onset of the mammoth

The road to Ronda: The automobile boneyard

tourism boom and a suddenly flowering economy for Spain – found themselves for the first time in their lives able to buy *un automóvil*. The villages and even medium-sized towns like Ronda had no automobile dealerships yet, so old Félix would take the bus from his mountain home down into Malaga, and there purchase a small Seat, the Spanish-built Fiat. To suggest that don Félix might be better off taking driving lessons first would be an assault on his honor and machismo, so he simply paid for the car and, after a few minutes of rudimentary instruction, unsteadily drove it away and headed for his mountain home. On one of the sharp curves, the totally inexperienced new driver would of course drive off the cliff. I can remember gazing down into one particular ravine on the winding mountain road from Malaga to Granada about 1969 or 1970 and counting at least a dozen car hulks at the bottom, some rusted, some with fresh paint jobs, and some at stages in between.

But all that was still in the future as my bus ground and strained its way up to Ronda. For now, the ravine bottoms were mercifully still pristine. The one-lane road would be widened to two lanes within two or three years, however, and as the twentieth century eventually approached its end, the Ronda *carretera* would metamorphize into a virtual superhighway. And the cliffbottom auto boneyards would disappear as drivers got the hang of it.

But now to my arrival in Ronda by bus. We crossed the 200-year-old Puente Nuevo spanning the mighty chasm which divides the ancient town into two parts and were let out in front of the plaza de toros. It was midafternoon and the sun was blasting down from a cloudless, deep blue sky. I was happy as a clam and began sightseeing immediately.

The bullring with its little museum was closed for siesta, so I walked over to the edge of the incredible cliff onto which much of the town either backs or faces, including the plaza de toros, "*lo más antigua de España.*" I remembered reading that in the pre-padding days when horses were killed in the ring, sometimes in great numbers, here in Ronda it was found to be most expedient to simply drag the horse carcasses the short distance from the plaza to the edge of the cliff, and tip them over. Nature's own Dead Horse Disposal. I could see vultures flying around down there, and I knew the story was that scavengers became so accustomed to the free meals back in the old days that their descendants still hung out there, intuitively, even after all the passing years.

I walked all through the old town and then later, as I was so wont to do, I ordered my *cerveza del día* at one of several old green metal tables beneath the striped awning of a little restaurant. There was no bar per se. Opposite was Ronda's wonderful old Plaza de Toros La Maestranza, basking in the golden sunlight of late afternoon. My thoughts were interrupted by a voice. A voice speaking in English with a German accent.

"You are worse than the American tourists at the Hofbrauhaus! Always you drink the beer!"

I looked around and groaned inwardly. "Wolfgang. What are you doing in Ronda?"

He sat down at my table. "I am visiting Spain. Ronda is a place of interest. It is an old Roman city."

"Yeah, right. And I'm the Emperor Trajan."

"That is stupid. You are not."

"Hey, you're right, Wolfgang. But whoever I am, you're following me. You got to the bus station in Malaga too late to get a seat on the bus I took, right?"

"I am not following you! I am visiting Spain!"

"Okay, okay." I sighed. "Look, you want a beer?"

"No. I am not a beer hall *Trinker*. I will have mineral water."

"Why pay for *water*, for God's sake?" I asked. "I thought you were cheap. Hell, you can get a glass of tap water – *wasser vom fass* – inside there, for nothing! And I guarantee you, you can't tell the difference!"

"There! You see! You are a barbarian! No European would drink tap water at the terrace. It is not done. It is what a... a... an *American* would do!"

"No. An American would drink beer. It's the same price as mineral water."

"Pah! Americans know nothing! You are all like big, friendly, stupid dogs wagging your tails and understanding nothing!"

"Well," I said, "I understand Spanish. Maybe not like a professor, but people seem to understand me. And we're in Spain, after all. I've never heard you speak more than a word or two in Spanish, Wolfgang."

"Pah! Spanish is not necessary! It is not an important language. *Untermenschen!*"

I decided to change the subject. "Did you know that Ronda is the home town of Spain's number one matador, Antonio Ordóñez?"

"Yes, I knew that," Wolfgang replied, then asked, "What means this? Number one?"

"It means he is the matador most people think is the best."

"So he always wins?"

"It's not really a case of winning or losing. It's how well one can perform the *toreo* with the bull," I said.

"So he does *not* always win!"

"He has been gored by bulls and carried from the ring, if that's what you mean."

Wolfgang looked triumphant. "So! He is *not* good! He lets himself be beaten by a stupid animal!"

I sighed. "Look, this is not getting us anywhere." I drained the rest of my beer and put the bottle on the table.

"So where does it get us?" asked the German. "Where are we, then?"

"*Somos los que estamos aquí*," I said.

What means this?" asked Wolfgang.

"It means, 'we are those who are here.'"

Wolfgang exploded. "That is ridiculous! Why would anyone say something so stupid? It means nothing!"

"It demonstrates the usage of the two verbs meaning *to be*," I explained. "Spanish taxi drivers find it very interesting. Say it, and they will always look at you twice in their rearview mirrors."

"Pah!" puffed Wolfgang. "This is too stupid to talk about!"

Well, it was indeed, so I left a brooding and still waterless Wolfgang and I went back to the Sierra de Montseny and my tree-planting.

CATALONIA / CATALUÑA / CATALUNYA

People sometimes ask me if I learned Catalan during my tree-planting days, and the answer is no. Under Franco, no regional languages or dialects were tolerated. Spain was to be a single, unified country, with one leader (*El Caudillo*), one party (the *Falange*), and one language (*Castellano*, or Spanish). Thus there were no newspapers, no radio, no signs, no nothing in Catalan. Only in *Castellano*. Where I worked, everything was in Spanish. So I never learned Catalan.

In Catalunya (this is the Catalan spelling of the Spanish word Cataluña) today, of course, street signs, names of public buildings, etc., are all in Catalan, and one can hear some, although not most, of the people on the streets speaking it. But one thing is for sure: *everybody* understands *Castellano*. And they had better, if they ever want to go anywhere outside their province. Elsewhere, Catalan is about as useful as, say, the Hawaiian language is in the U.S. The land area of Catalunya is smaller than that of South Carolina; in other words, small. To me, Catalunya is not much more than Greater Barcelona. And yet the dream of many is full independence.

Today I have some constant reminders of the old Catalonia/Cataluña/Catalunya in both my home and my office. On a wall of the latter is a three-by-four-foot photographic blowup of me and some of my fellow tree-planters on a Catalan mountainside, made in 1960 – a scroungy-looking bunch, I can tell you. But I did have a full head of bushy blond hair. Sigh.

DON'T MESS WITH THE GUARDIA CIVIL

Aficionados who went to Spanish *corridas* during the Franco years will recall that there was always a contingent of Guardia Civil present, normally seated as a bloc in the *grada sombra*. In deference to the crowded conditions of the bullring, the guardia's usual shoulder-slung carbines were left at the *cuartel*, supplanted for the afternoon by holstered pistols. Pretty good duty it seemed to me, particularly as I never witnessed a time when their services as enforcers of the law were required during an afternoon at the *Fiesta Nacional*.

Michener, however, reports that on at least one occasion in Sevilla, with a bullring riot apparently incipient, the unit of guardia present filed down from their seats and entered the arena, whereupon they formed a circle facing outward and methodically drew their pistols, pointing them at *el público*. The disturbance in the plaza ceased instantly, for no one had the slightest doubt that the guardia would have fired into the crowd, had order not been restored.

My first encounter with the Guardia Civil occurred at the border railroad station in Irún, across the frontier with France and just outside of San Sebastián. I had met another American college student, a pleasant fellow named Nat, on the train from Toulouse, and, for capturing memorable scenes of his adventure, he had among his belongings a camera and an egg-carton-like container of the big, cumbersome flash bulbs of those days. A commercial art student, I relied on a sketchbook and rapidograph pen.

At Hendaye, on the French side, everybody got off the train and walked through the French border control, then on to the Spanish *aduana* post. There was a reason why we walked, rather than staying on the train: the French railroad tracks, as in the rest of Western Europe, were of a wider gauge than those of Spain. The high class international trains with sleeping cars would stop at the border and have their wheels bogeyed to fit the Spanish tracks, but ordinary trains such as the one I and my friend rode simply terminated at the frontier, requiring all passengers to leave the French train, trudge across the imaginary dotted line with our belongings, and board a Spanish train on the other side – after first passing through the *aduana española*.

Inside the customs building, a small, stucco edifice with a red tiled roof, my friend Nat and I presented our passports to the policeman-border guard wearing a gray uniform with red trim, and after stamping our documents he waved us on. However, a gray-green-clad fellow sporting a black patent leather hat put out his hand and ordered us to open our luggage. This, of course, was the Guardia Civil.

And guess what the guardia found? *Bombas!* Yes, bombs – at least, according to the mustachioed sergeant who was digging though my friend's belongings. He opened the flash bulb carton and held aloft one of the illegal weapons, for all *el mundo* to see: an egg-sized glass device with many tiny wires clearly visible inside, and with an obvious plug-end of some sort. *Bombas!*

We spent several minutes explaining to the guardia that the flash bulbs were *para sacar fotografías*, and had nothing got do with a cabal of terrorism against the Franco regime. Nat finally took a flash picture of the man, in way of demonstration, at which time the guardia started for his gun, but then relaxed as he realized what it was all about. He barked at us to move on, his gruff demeanor a cover, of course, for his embarrassment. (The fool! We were now poised to photograph Franco's top secret Radium Furnaces, shovel-fed by Republican POWs still enslaved since the Spanish Civil War! No, not really.)

I also remember a time when I was trying to hitch a ride from inland Cataluña to the coast. I'd had no luck during the late afternoon hours and it was now dark as I was walking along a dirt highway, when I heard a car coming. I automatically turned and put out my and, not in the American thumb-out manner but in the continental-wave sort of way. With much scrunching of tires and great clouds of dust, a small, Spanish-built Seat slid to a stop several yards down the road. I ran along and got in, learning soon that the driver was a Spanish student returning home from a university in Paris. Even I knew that, in those days, if a Spanish student type had access to a car, much less university in Paris, he had to be somebody special. All I said was *gracias*. Then we roared off like a bat out of hell, in another cloud of dust.

Once you come down from the mountainous area of Cataluña, everything gets relatively flat pretty quick. And while the road we were traveling was a dirt one it was smooth and well-surfaced and we were probably going 100 kph through the night. A few miles further on, our headlamps picked up a pair of gray-green-clad Guardia Civil walking along the road, their carbines slung over their shoulders, and they waved for us to stop. What would've happened had we not stopped? Communications were fairly primitive in a lot of ways, but if we had ignored their call to halt, and then if, somehow, their buddies *had* subsequently caught us – I shuddered at the thought. In any case, we slid to a stop in yet one more billowing of dust and the two rifle-toting guardia came up to each front window and leaned into the car. They had questions.

"*A donde van?*"

"To Arenys de Mar, on the coast," the driver replied.

"*Porqué?*"

"To let off this person I picked up."

"*Y a donde va usted?*"

"To Barcelona. My family lives there."

"*Y este señor?*"

I told them I was an *estadounidense* and was going to Arenys to meet some friends for a weekend on the beach. We had no money and would probably just sleep on the beach.

"*Su pasaporte!*"

I gave it to the guardia peering through the passenger-side window and he studied it carefully before handing it back to me.

"*Vayan!*" he cried, waving his hand in the direction of the empty road ahead. Obeying, my driver friend pulled away, uncharacteristically carefully, until we were around a bend, at which time he floorboarded it.

The guardia's job, among other things, was to know what was going on in their district at all times. If there were foreigners present, Franco's minions were supposed to know at all times who they were and what they were up to. They also helped enforce important laws, such as that church-inspired ban on two-piece swimsuits at the beach. But their whole world came crashing down around their heads with the incredible tourism boom of the late sixties. Suddenly there were *hundreds of thousands* of foreigners in Spain, and not only were there bikinis everywhere, there were *topless* ladies in abundance! What were the guardia supposed to do – arrest or shoot them all? Throngs who were bringing in billions of much-needed pesetas to impoverished Spain? Franco's dictatorship was not *that* extreme; the tourists won, the guardia backed off. And that, to my mind, was the end of the fierce image of Spain's Guardia Civil.

Today one can occasionally see the Guardia Civil in their traditional uniforms, but nowdays it's most likely to be at a national holiday function involving a parade, or perhaps a special church service with VIPs in attendance. Pairs of guardia in Land Rover type vehicles, not foot patrols, still keep an eye on the highways of Spain, but the ominous black patent leather hats are gone, replaced by more democratic-looking headgear, and the more relaxed authority figures no longer stop cars to question the inhabitants randomly.

But even if they did, I suspect they would these days know the difference between a flash bulb and a bomb.

A JEWEL THIEF IN MY GROUP

Like many other people, when it comes to thinking about criminals who are guilty as sin, yet who escape punishment thanks to a slick lawyer, I have often gotten angry. Yet I once found myself in the uncomfortable position of having to try to help a jewel thief.

It was on Spain's Costa del Sol, and Generalísimo Franco was the dictator. The crime rate in Spain was probably the lowest in Western Europe at the time and crooks didn't mess around with *El Caudillo's* boys. Rights and other niceties seemed to be not that big a deal in those days on the Iberian Peninsula. That's what makes this particular episode that much more memorable, as a member of one of my groups pulled a jewel heist there.

My gaggle of business machine salespeople, qualifiers of a sales goal campaign, and their spouses, were lodged at a hotel directly facing the beach and the blue Mediterranean. We were in the Hotel Pez Espada just outside Torremolinos, then the only resort on the 75-mile coast which would a few years later look like Miami Beach.

I was in the hotel manager's office on the afternoon of my group's second day of a one-week visit. He and I were talking when his secretary suddenly burst in, quite agitated.

"*La Policía!*" she shouted. "*Están en número cuatro-veinte-cuatro! Ellos quieren Señor Hosch!*"

I looked at the girl, then at the hotel manager, at a loss as to what I should say. The police were in room 424 and wanted me? But why? There was nothing for me to do but go and find out. The manager, a Polish national who wanted as little as possible to do with the police, shrugged and looked fearful, but didn't accompany me, rushing to his room to hastily rearrange his sock drawer.

In 424 I found five people. Two of them were stonefaced, trenchcoated men wearing Borsolino-type hats. The police. Like characters in a bad B movie. The third was a thiry-fivish man I recognized as a loudmouth bigshot-wannabee from my group – a salesman, I recalled, from New Orleans, whose name was Joe LaCosta. Wiry, medium height, black hair, permanent five-o'clock'shadow. He was handcuffed to a chair with arm rests and looked scared to death – a departure from his usual obnoxious demeanor.

The others in the room were Mr, and Mrs. Charlie Bellino, also members of my group and, like Joe LaCosta, from New Orleans.

The taller of the two policemen, a thin, blond man, addressed me. He told me in Spanish that a jewelry store in Torremolinos had been robbed the day previous of a large quantity of gold rings with gemstone settings, and that said jewelry had been found to be in the possession of Señor LaCosta. He gestured toward a dresser top, which was covered with rings studded with emeralds, sapphires, rubies, diamonds, *y así sucesivamente*, as the Spanish say, meaning et cetera. The loot, the trenchcoated one explained, had been found in a dresser drawer here in Señor LaCosta's room, beneath his underwear. Obviously, the hotel maid had reported the discovery. I looked at the handcuffed La Costa, and told him what the policemen had said.

"I told him I don't know nuthin' about this!" Joe yelled. "I didn't steal nuthin'!"

The cop then told me that Joe had at first said that he didn't know how the jewelry had gotten into his drawer. Then when the police announced they had found a few more such pieces in Mr. and Mrs. Bellino's room, also tucked away beneath underwear, and Mr. and Mrs. Bellino had then said they'd been given the rings by Mr. LaCosta, who told them, "Hey, take dese home to y' kids!" – well, then Joe had remembered that, oh yeah, he had gotten the stuff, but by God, he'd paid for it.

The trenchcoated cop in charge, whose name was, predictably, Garcia, told me that several full trays of rings had disappeared from the jewelry shop after a young salesperson had foolishly left them on the counter with three Americans, two men and a woman, while she, the employee, had gone into the back room to answer the telephone. When she returned, the two men and the woman were gone, and so were the rings. Agent García said he had no doubt that she could identify these three people. Neither did I.

The Bellinos, though, were apparently ready to go the extra half mile for their friend Joe. The man defended Joe, sort of, describing him as just a poor guy who was trying to have a good time after his crummy wife had walked out on him. They felt sure he had paid for the rings.

García the cop put an end to all this quickly and effectively. He asked me to tell the Bellinos that unless they told him the truth now, not only would Señor LaCosta begin his rotting process in the local hellhole which served as a jail, but so would they.

The Bellinos looked at each other and deliberated for three seconds.

"He did it!" they both shouted, pointing at Joe.

The detective smiled, and in a few minutes, Joe and his accomplices were escorted from the room.

I haven't been required to check out the jail in Torremolinos recently, but at that time it was located on the deceptively idyllic little Plaza de los Naranjos, in the heart of the old town. I later entered the jail to visit Joe; the door from the square opened into a small office with little else than a desk, behind which sat a fat, uniformed policeman. A large metal hoop with a bunch of keys on it lay on the desk.

When I first saw Joe in his new home, he was a cowering, frightened wreck, a mere shell of his former cocky self. Secretly I was glad, but as I was now accompanied by two company officials – Joe's superiors and my clients – I had to keep a straight face.

The jail's one and only cell looked like something from the Spanish Inquisition. The door was rounded, maybe three feet high, and iron bars closed it off. The cell was windowless and, hence, dark. Joe was gripping the bars in classic gangster movie style, and his expression was panic-stricken.

"You guys gotta get me outa here!" Joe yelled in that funny Yat accent of New Orleans that sometimes sounds almost Brooklynese. "Hey, do you realize that if I don't spring for the cost of a meal, I don't eat? That fat slob out there has my wallet, and whatever I order from that greasy spoon next door, he deducts from my supply of cash!"

We shook our heads and commiserated.

"But that ain't all!" Joe continued. "See dese crumbums?" he gestured with a thumb at the other three male figures in the cell with him, gentlemen the jailer later told me about. One, it seemed, was a drunk – notorious, but common. The next was a fifteen-year-old *espontáneo*, someone who illegally leaps into the bullring and tries to fight the bull before the gathered crowd, in an effort to catch the eye of a potential *patrón* who can then get his imagined career on track. The third was a hotel bellhop who had punched an American woman tourist in the nose.

"If I don't buy them breakfast, lunch and dinner, too, they beat me up!" Joe bleated. "I'm going broke, man! You gotta get me outa here!"

Costa de Sol: Our very own jewel thief

Well, I have already said I had been charged with getting Joe off. In retrospect, I guess I'm not much of a legal mouthpiece, because he remained incarcerated for the several days required by Spanish law, before bail would even be considered. All the while, Joe's superiors kept pushing me to do something, but although I visited the jail daily, I made no progress. I spoke with the presiding judge; nada. As agent García had predicted, Joe rotted in jail, although the Bellinos, now saddled with the mantle of ratfinks, didn't.

The rotting process unfortunately did not last long enough. After almost a week, Joe was entitled to go free, provided he could pay a staggering bond, which he just managed to do, with the help of borrowed money from his employers. If everything had gone according to schedule, my group would have been gone by the time Joe got out, but as we were traveling via a supplemental carrier's charter flight service, our departure time could vary up to twenty-four hours.

This departure pushed that limit, so Joe made it to the Malaga airport just in time for the return flight home. He was all grins, his old self again, full of stories about how he made monkeys of those stupid Spanish cops, and vividly describing how he was so much smarter than everybody else. His buddies laughed and toasted him with drinks from the airport bar. The younger women, or "chicks" as old Joe called them, fawned over him like he was a movie idol.

It made me sick, but then I decided that when Joe LaCosta got back to New Orleans and thought back on his trip to Spain and could only conjure up visions of an eight-by-eight, darkened concrete cell and the small bail bond fortune he had forfeited to the Spanish court – and still owed to his bosses – maybe some of his bravado would sour.

And if these thoughts didn't do it, perhaps being told by his firm two weeks later that his services were no longer required, did.

TANGIER NOCTURNE

A day trip to Tangier, Morocco, eventually became a must-do excursion for groups in southern Spain, but the very first time I went there I was a young man on my own. I took the ferry from Algeciras, and upon arrival in the North African port a couple of hours later, I and all my fellow ferry passengers were besieged by locals wearing *jellabas*, the long robes in the traditional arab style, offering accommodations at hotels and pensions. I was of course on the lookout for the latter, in the interest of economy, and so when a young arab boy in his own mini-robe called out, *"Pensión! Pensión!"* I questioned him about the price. Satisfied, I said, *"Vámanos!"* (everybody in Tangier spoke Spanish as well as Arabic) and we were off, the boy lugging my suitcase which, although small, appeared big in his grasp.

He led me away from the pier and up the hill toward the medina, or old arab quarter. Soon we were traversing cobblestone streets which got progressively narrower, until we were in a sort of alleyway about four feet across. There were plenty of people about, all wearing *jellabas*. At last we came to the pension, probably a former private home, which was built in the traditional arab style of the three-story building with arched, balconied floors surrounding an inner courtyard. This may sound attractive, but it was not: the place was a dirty dump. But the price was right, so I took it, paying in advance for two nights.

I spent a couple of days walking all over Tangier – the modern French-style city as well as the old medina, dodging laden camels and burros. At the end of the second day, I turned in for the night. My windowless room had been subdivided from a larger space; the back wall and one side wall were part of the original stone building, while the other two walls and the door were made of half-inch-thick plywood. The lock on the door was nothing more than an eye-hook of the type people had on their screened doors in the U.S.

In the middle of the night I was suddenly awakened by the sound of two men shouting in Arabic in the room on the other side of my plywood wall, which was really only a nine-foot-high partition, as it did not reach the ceiling. The shouting progressed to a fight: I could hear blows being landed and cries of *"Oof!"* and *"Arrgh!"*, and at one point the men obviously crashed into the dividing wall, buckling it in alarmingly and causing cracking, splitting-wood sounds. Then there was a long, anguished cry, *"Ahhhhh!"*, followed by a thud. Like a body hitting the floor. Silence. Then I heard the other room's door open and close, and footsteps fade down the outer passageway.

I lay there in my narrow bed, now wide awake, and I continued to do so until I could see gray, pre-dawn light beginning to show through the cracks around my plywood door. I hurridly packed up my meager belongings and, having already paid for my room, blew the joint. And Tangier as well.

REFLECTION

It was a Golden Age in many ways, at least for me. And I think it is ironic that I can clearly remember thinking one day in Spain at the time that while all this was so wonderful, I had a feeling I'd better really try to absorb as much as I could, right then, because it was probably going to change greatly in the years to come.

How right I was.

THE END

Printed in the United States
By Bookmasters